PRESENTING

Ouida Sebestyen

Twayne's United States Authors Series
Young Adult Authors

Patricia J. Campbell, General Editor

TUSAS 648

Ouida Sebestyen
Courtesy of Ouida Sebestyen.

PRESENTING

Ouida
Sebestyen

Virginia R. Monseau

Twayne Publishers • New York
Maxwell Macmillan Canada • Toronto
Maxwell Macmillan International • New York Oxford Singapore Sydney

Twayne's United States Authors Series No. 648

Presenting Ouida Sebestyen
Virginia R. Monseau

Twayne Publishers   Maxwell Macmillan Canada Inc.
Macmillan Publishing Company   1200 Eglinton Avenue East
866 Third Avenue   Suite 200
New York, New York 10022   Don Mills, Ontario M3C 3N1

Library of Congress Cataloging-in-Publication Data

Monseau, Virginia R., 1941–
    Presenting Ouida Sebestyen / Virginia R. Monseau.
        p. cm.—(Twayne's United States authors series. Young
    adult authors)
    Includes bibliographical references and index.
    ISBN 0-8057-8224-9
    1. Sebestyan, Ouida—Criticism and interpretation. 2. Young adult
fiction, America—History and criticism. I. Title. II. Series.
PS3569.E2865Z78   1994
813'.54—dc20   94-3681
                                                             CIP

The paper used in this publication meets the minimum requirements of American National Standards for Information Sciences—Permanence of Paper for Printed Library Materials. ANSI Z3948-1984. ∞

10 9 8 7 6 5 4 3 2 1 (hc)
10 9 8 7 6 5 4 3 2 1 (pb)

Printed in the United States of America

For
Paul, Michele, and Jennifer

Contents

Foreword

The advent of Twayne's Young Adult Author Series in 1985 was a response to the growing stature and value of adolescent literature and the lack of serious critical evaluation of the new genre. The first volume in the series was heralded as marking the coming-of-age of young adult fiction.

The aim of the series is twofold. First, it enables young readers to research the work of their favorite authors, and to see them as real people. Each volume is written in a lively, readable style and attempts to present in an attractive, accessible format a vivid portrait of the author as a person.

Second, the series provides teachers and librarians with insights and background material for promoting and teaching young adult novels. Each of the biocritical studies is a serious literary analysis of one author's work (or one sub-genre within young adult literature), with attention to plot structure, theme, character, setting, and imagery. In addition, many of the series writers delve deeper into the creative writing process by tracking down early drafts or unpublished manuscripts by their subject authors, consulting with their editors or other mentors, and examining influences from literature, film, or social movements.

Many of the contributing authors of the series are among the leading scholars and critics of adolescent literature. Some are even young adult novelists themselves. Most of the studies are based on extensive interviews with the subject author, and each includes an exhaustive study of his or her work. Although the general format is the same, the individual volumes are uniquely shaped by their subjects, and each brings a different perspective to the classroom.

The goal of the series is to produce a succinct but comprehensive study of the life and art of every leading young adult author writing in the United States today. The books trace how that art has been accepted by readers and critics, evaluate its place in the developing field of adolescent literature, and—perhaps most important—inspire a reading and re-reading of this quality fiction that speaks so directly to young people about their life experiences.

PATRICIA J. CAMPBELL, General Editor

Acknowledgments

I am extremely grateful to Ouida Sebestyen for her gracious cooperation in the preparation of this manuscript. Not only did she make my three-day visit to Boulder, Colorado, a joy, but she also gave me access to many of her treasured photographs, letters, and other mementos related to her work as a novelist for young adults. Any otherwise undocumented facts and quotations in this book can be attributed to notes and tape recordings from our extended interview, which took place in August 1992.

Special thanks are also due to Melanie Kroupa, Ouida Sebestyen's long-time editor, who provided me with valuable information about the evolution of the author's work and put me in touch with others who could aid my research. Her prompt attention to all of my requests is greatly appreciated.

I am indebted to Megan Tingley and Erica Lombard of Little, Brown and Company, who provided me with access to files essential to the completion of this project. I am also appreciative of the kindness and expertise of Karen Nelson Hoyle, curator of the Kerlan Collection, housed in the University of Minnesota's Walter Library. Finally, I thank my daughter Jennifer, who served as my research assistant and technical consultant throughout this project. That she was prompted to reread all of Ouida Sebestyen's novels after reading this manuscript is testimony to the quality of Sebestyen's work.

Chronology

1924   Ouida Glenn Dockery born 13 February in Vernon, Texas.

1941   Graduates from Vernon High School, Vernon, Texas.

1942   Works for two years as a civilian mechanic at Victory Field, a training field for aviation cadets outside of Vernon.

1944   Attends University of Colorado at Boulder for one summer.

1945   Writes *The Dwelling Place*, her first novel (unpublished).

1950   Publishes short story "Children Are a Blessing" in *Everywoman*, a Canadian magazine.

1951   Publishes "Children Are a Blessing" in *Mother and Home* in England.

1960   Marries Hungarian refugee, Adam Sebestyen. Lives in San Anselmo, California, during the marriage.

1961   Her son Corbin is born.

1966   Divorced from Adam Sebestyen. Moves to Boulder, Colorado.

1968   Publishes short story "Words by Heart" in *Ingenue*.

1979 Publishes *Words by Heart*, named a *New York Times* Best Book; a *School Library Journal* Best Book; an A.L.A. Notable Children's Book; an A.L.A. Best Book for Young Adults; one of *Learning Magazine*'s Ten Best Books of the Year; a Library of Congress Children's Book of the Year; and recipient of the International Reading Association's Children's Book Award.

1980 Publishes *Far from Home*.

1982 Publishes *IOU's*.

1985 *Words by Heart* televised, PBS.

1985 Publishes *On Fire*.

1988 Publishes *The Girl in the Box*.

1990 Publishes her first play, "Holding Out," in *Center Stage*.

1993 Moves from Boulder, Colorado, to Lockhart, Texas.

1994 Publishes *Out of Nowhere*.

1. A Loner, but Never Lonely

The old Volkswagen bus rolled to a stop at the entrance to the Holiday Inn. Out hopped a sprightly woman in a plaid shirt, khaki pants, and tennis shoes, a cloud of silver hair framing her youthful face. I remember thinking, "She really hasn't changed much since I last saw her, five years ago." In April 1987 Ouida Sebestyen had been our guest author at Youngstown State University's annual English Festival, where she graciously and enthusiastically spoke to throngs of students, teachers, librarians, and parents over a three-day period.

During the course of our two days together in Boulder in August 1992, I was to learn not only that Sebestyen's grace and enthusiasm are still intact, but also that she is a woman possessed of an abiding inner strength coupled with a sense of being at peace with the world. When I arrived in town the preceding day and spoke to her on the phone, she had suggested that we conduct our interview outdoors—perhaps taking a walk or having a picnic, since the weather was so beautiful. I had immediately agreed but was nagged by the thought of dragging my tape recorder and other paraphernalia along. Forever the city girl, I was to learn a few lessons about the important things in life.

Willing to endure any discomfort but goose bumps, I had pulled a cotton sweater over my T-shirt before leaving my hotel room to meet her—braced for the crisp but sunny Colorado morning. Ouida Sebestyen apparently didn't worry about such things, as there was no sweater in sight when I climbed into the VW bus next to the driver, her son Corbin. She jumped in the back, assuring me that was where she preferred to ride, and asked me if I'd like to go up into the mountains to walk and talk. Corbin said he would be glad to drop us off and come back for us later.

It was then that I really began to learn about Ouida Sebestyen, as conversation turned to our mode of transportation. It seems that she and Corbin had bought the old VW bus years before for two hundred dollars, and that the two of them had worked together to put it in running condition. They were obviously proud of their accomplishment, bragging that Corbin frequently drives it back and forth between Colorado and California, where he works. Sebestyen made a point of saying that she doesn't mind being alone when Corbin is away. In fact, she rather enjoys it. "I think I'm just a loner," she says. "That's my personality. It doesn't bother me. Sometimes I actually prefer myself, and animals, and plants—and then people—maybe in that order." But she quickly adds, "I *am* a people person, but I'm more a natural observer than a participant or leader, and maybe I need that sense of standing back and watching. Anyway, I don't ever feel lonely."

An only child herself, she frequently writes about only children in her novels: Salty Yeager in *Far from Home*, Stowe Garrett in *IOU's*, Jackie McGee in *The Girl in the Box*, and Harley Nunn in *Out of Nowhere*. And she gives to these young protagonists her own strength of character, her independence and will to survive.

We decided on Chautauqua Park as the setting for our interview that day, and the scene was idyllic. The crisp early morning air had warmed to the mid-seventies; as we walked the trails she pointed out various plants and landmarks, talking about her life as a child growing up in Vernon, Texas. Having lived in Boulder for the last twenty-six years, she had decided to move back to Texas; in fact, she had recently returned from looking for a piece of land somewhere in the Hill Country there, a simpler place where she could grow more plants and feel closer to nature. Admitting that it would be hard to leave Boulder, she added, "You have to stretch yourself occasionally, and this feels like the time. Every twenty years or so you need to do something crazy."

Her life as a child in Texas was the inspiration for *Words by Heart*, and the Sills family represent people she knew when she

I'm sharing the tub with a cooling watermelon on my uncle's old Texas farm. (The seeds of the Sills' rent-house in *Words by Heart?*)

was growing up there. The character of Lena, for example, grew out of Sebestyen's admiration for her aunt. The entire book, she admits, "was a long goodby [sic] to [her] father" with whom she had shared "thirty-eight close and loving years."[1] Though she has written a companion piece to the novel with *On Fire*, many of her young readers ask for a sequel to *Words by Heart*; but so far she has resisted writing one, preferring instead to tell other stories.

Reveling in my favorite things: home, plants, pets, and coveralls (a cutoff version).

She hasn't dismissed the idea completely, though; when I suggested that moving back to Texas might reinspire her, she smiled and agreed that might be possible.

Sebestyen's creativity took many forms as she was growing up. She loved to write plays in which her friends and young relatives would perform, and she enjoyed "dressing up" in costumes and old clothes. "All the misfit kids in our town gravitated to my house," she says, "where we wrote songs, poetry, and skits—and 'tried on' endless roles, hunting who we were and wanted to be."

Her childhood in Texas was a happy one, surrounded by loving parents and other relatives, and this experience is mirrored in several of her novels. As her books indicate, family is very important to her, and she speaks warmly of the years spent in a three-generation household.

> My mother and my son and I filled each other's spaces when my
> divorce and her widowhood turned us into a three-generation
> family, without a home or livelihood but undoubtedly rich in
> everything except money. It was in the two-mother household
> which all of us had created together that I began to write des-
> perately in a last try for success before I gave up the crazy
> dream and got a real job. Supported on either side by two gener-
> ations whose faith in me divided all the hardships into thirds,
> how could I help but write about the wonders of being family?
> ("Family Matters," 2)

Given her own secure family background, Sebestyen is puzzled
by her penchant for writing about homeless boys like Salty
Yeager and Sammy Haney. She is equally uncertain about why so
many of her young male protagonists are searching for their
fathers. Perhaps these characters reflect her unconscious concern
about her own son's growing up in an all-female household.
Certainly, they are not reflective of Sebestyen's childhood: as
mentioned earlier, she was very close to her own father, who was
a teacher, and when she was younger she loved to travel with her

Marie has been a dear friend for sixty-four years; Lassie shared my
teens. Both tolerated my bouts of "dressing up" and "play acting."

A hapless little cousin escapes with me into another time, place, and character. Lots of "pretend" memories from this time to use in *Far from Home*—and obliquely in every book, of course.

parents. In fact, when given the choice of using savings to go to college or to take a trip with her parents, she remembers saying without hesitation, "Let's pack."

My parents at an old sawmill in Arizona. Traveling the West with them—and perhaps a friend and a dog—was heaven on wheels.

Sebestyen spent only a short time in college, at the University of Colorado; she decided it would be more exciting to leave school and work on airplanes. It was wartime, so women were needed in industry to perform work ordinarily done in those days by men. She worked for about two years, doing outside maintenance on airplanes, working alongside the "old guys," as she calls them. When the younger men returned from the war, however, she was laid off, so she turned her attention to writing.

Her desire to build things hasn't diminished. It continues to grow alongside her desire to write. She confides:

> One of my two dreams is to have a piece of land where I can have more pets, big trees, gardens, a workshop, and space. I would love to restore an old house, or build a new one from scratch—being one of the carpenters, bricklayers, cabinet-makers,

painters and landscapers myself. Then—after I've gone around the world—I'd like to settle there, plant an orchard and make patchwork quilts. And every so often, sit in an audience that is watching a movie made from a book I've written. Because the

My parents buy two acres outside our Texas town, hoping to build a house for them and a studio for me. Hard, wonderful work at Wind Hill!

second dream, of course, is to grow as a writer, to move readers to laugh and cry and recognize themselves, to give them other worlds to live in. It is frightening to write for children, because they are looking so hard for answers and examples and confirmation. But if I'm lucky, and dig deeply down into myself, maybe I can find ways to remind them of their strengths and specialness, and nourish the marvelous impudent hope and idealism and optimism that they have.[2]

After her divorce from Adam Sebestyen in 1966, determined to continue writing, Sebestyen took a variety of jobs to help make ends meet, as she, her mother, and her son set up their three-generation household. "When the money ran out," she says, "I kept children in my home [like Annie Garrett in *IOU's*], hired out as a housekeeper, mowed lawns, upholstered furniture, and kept a church nursery (until I took the kids wading in the creek in their Sunday clothes)" ("Misspent Youth," 2).

This sort of Sunday-School adventure seemed to typify the Ouida Sebestyen I was coming to know. Lucky enough to spend a second day with her, I found myself once again in the beautiful

The four geese marching across a green lawn stopped traffic as Wind Hill becomes a beauty spot.

A change of plans. Enter romance. I marry, and a year later share Christmas with a son!

Celebrating an award with a bewhiskered Corbin and a gingersnap. How the years have flown!

Rocky Mountains overlooking Boulder. As we picked our way among the jagged rocks and prickly cacti—she in her bare feet, carrying her shoes, and I firmly protected by my trusty Keds—we stopped to watch some mountain climbers in the distance. Sebestyen talked about the excitement of trying something dangerous, reminiscing about the time she rode in a hot-air balloon—which landed in a tangle of telephone wires. "Somebody saw us, and we suddenly heard all these sirens coming," she remembered. "The police came, the sheriff came, the paramedics came." Fortunately, no one was injured. The incident did not frighten Sebestyen one bit: she calls ballooning a "gentle" experience and doesn't discount the possibility of trying skydiving someday.

This spirit of adventure and eagerness to meet life head-on are fascinating qualities in a woman who, on the surface, seems rather shy and reserved. Her long-time editor, Melanie Kroupa, describes her as a "fragile rock," and says that she has often drawn on Sebestyen's inner strength and positive outlook in difficult times. These qualities might very well be what make Sebestyen's books so popular with young readers. Noting that

I recover from whirlwind book promotion tours with help from Neptune and the Rocky Mountains.

After all the role-testing, this turns out to be the real me.

motherhood was the turning point of both her life and her career, she sees a distinct similarity between writing and parenting:

> Having children and writing books for them are both acts of faith and giving. Parents and writers make the first leap when they choose to love what doesn't yet exist but is coming and will someday be. . . . Writers and parents put a lot of energy and time into earning trust, being fair, and keeping a tolerant dialogue going between generations. . . . A book written for young readers has to come out of the child in the writer as well as the adult, from the same memory-place where parents find empathy. Both parents and writers need to do more than hold the mirror up to life for those they're speaking to. They need to tilt the mirror so it catches light, and suggests not only how life is, but how it ought to be. ("Family Matters," 2–3)

When we think about characters like Ben and Lena Sills, Salty Yeager and Tom Buckley, Annie and Stowe Garrett, Jackie McGee—and even Tater and Sammy Haney—it becomes clear that Sebestyen, too, knows her words by heart. Her fictional creations mirror her philosophy of living, and her readers are richer for it. "To read Ouida Sebestyen is to feel deeply the power of good," one reviewer has written.[3] But the good we feel is not the result of excessive sentimentalism, nor does it come from the pathos of sorrow or pity; rather, it comes from a glimpse of ourselves as we'd like to be, as we know we can be—morally strong, upright, and courageous. She gives us, as readers, the desire to strive for perfection, perhaps to return from whence we came. In a world that sometimes seems so full of evil, indifference, and despair, Ouida Sebestyen reminds us that we are our own best hope.

2. Making Magic

At the Children's Literature Association Conference in June 1990, Ouida Sebestyen told the story of a serious little boy who once asked her, "Would you comment on the words you use?" Thinking he wanted to talk about "the beautiful English language," she thought, "Of course I'd love to talk about words!" But as she began to reply, he added, "I mean the bad ones. The cursing." Reflecting on this young boy's comment, Sebestyen told her audience:

> Actually, I'm not able to think of words as good or bad, acceptable or vulgar. They're my tools. Carpenters don't have vulgar or polite tools. So I collect and use sharp chisel words, and rubber-mallet words that can whomp the bejabbers out of things without leaving a mark. I love using words that are like slabs of redwood—rare—with five hundred years of time, history, seasons, changes captured in their very fibers. I love cement and gravel words I can stir and pour and trowel into sentences that will outlive me.[1]

Accusing Ouida Sebestyen of using vulgar language in her books seems a bit far-fetched. True, Mrs. Chism does utter one or two expletives in *Words by Heart*, and unsavory characters toss off some racial and ethnic slurs in *On Fire*. But Sebestyen makes an important distinction among these words, as she reported to her young interrogator: "I don't use swearwords, at least not out loud. Do you? No? Then we're lucky—we have more imaginative, strong ways to express our feelings and ideas than those people in my books did" ("Balancing the Books," 41).

To Sebestyen, weaving words together into a fascinating story is "making magic." This is what she has set out to do throughout her life as a writer. "I want my readers to go away with a sense of wonder and magic," she says, "great mystery of life and all that." But the magic does not happen easily, and Sebestyen is the first to admit that writing can be a messy process. "I always have myriads of papers everywhere and keep making little stacks," she says. "I spread them out around the couch and keep going back to look at them."

Sebestyen wants beginning writers to know that writing is a painstaking process, and she has kept careful notes to share. "First comes the idea," she says, "maybe only vague feelings of a time or place or a character." She continues:

> For awhile you stir them, walk around them, trying different combinations, waiting for something to come alive and seize your imagination. This is the point where people ask you, "Why are you sitting there with your eyes closed? Why aren't you working?"

"You begin to make notes to yourself," she explains, "to get the thoughts down on paper, so that they start to have a shape you can work with." She stresses that writers rarely grab a blank sheet of paper and start a book without this kind of preliminary work.

As evidence of her own process, Sebestyen has pages and pages of notes, many of them written on the back of old manuscripts or her son's school papers. Always concerned about preserving our natural resources, she admits,

> A small objective part of me thinks we already chop down too many trees and spew out too many books and magazines and newspapers and reports-in-triplicate, full of chitchat and ephemera—mine included. I catch that part of me thinking, Well, I haven't planted a tree today, but at least I'm writing the Great American Novel on the back of my junk mail." ("Balancing the Books," 39)

One of her lists, for example, contains a litany of character names that she brainstormed while working on *Far from Home*. Another, entitled "The Roaring Twenties—The Golden Decade" lists slang common to the time ("the berries," "cat's meow," "heebie-jeebies"), as well as common pastimes (flagpole sitting, marathon dancing, roller skating) that she might have used in her book. "Details must be chosen with care," she says "so that each one adds something. Even simple things like the characters' names can be used to help you get the effect you want." In this case, Sebestyen listed magazines of the period, radio shows, songs, department stores—even some old 1920s jokes that she used in *Far from Home*: someone says, "Moronia thinks the postage stamp is a dance," and someone responds, "Well, letter"; or someone says, "I'm mute," and someone answers, "You don't say." Sebestyen even categorizes many of the slang expressions and historic or cultural events by year, so that she can be precise in detail as she shapes plot and characters.

Discussing character development, she says, "Either I see a person and that person becomes a character, or I'm fiddling with a character and I see a person and say, 'Oh, yeah, that's how he looks, or that's how he would talk.'" She continues:

> Characters keep growing, and as you write, you get to know them better. They reveal themselves sometimes in ways you don't expect. And you think, "Hey, I didn't know that about you. Wow." And at the end you think, "This character is like a friendship. Someone slowly peels off layers until you know a different person from the one you first met."

She's always concerned, too, about how setting and time affect her characters. One of her lists, again for *Far from Home*, fits characters into historical events and cultural trends:

- Roseann's folks lost all their money in 1929 crash—she can't depend on them to pay her way.
- All Salty's relations died in flu epidemic of 1918—all but Dovie and Mam.

- Tom was gassed in World War I—came home married to nurse—she left him three years later—he resumed friendship with Dovie.
- Jo is first to bob her hair, wear short skirts, silk stockings—She is rebel, shocking, suspect.

As far as setting is concerned, all of Sebestyen's books except *The Girl in the Box* take place in locales where she herself has lived. This familiarity with the physical setting enables her to concentrate more on historical and cultural details as she weaves them into her stories.

In addition to stressing the important relationship between character and setting, Sebestyen also believes that a writer needs to know, from the outset, how a book will end, even if the exact details are not clear early on. "In a strong book everything, from the first page on, should lead up to that ending," she says. One of her lists for *Far from Home* entitled "Thinking Ahead" contains notes to herself about conversations certain characters will have with one another as the book progresses.

Sebestyen's endings are often the subject of discussion, as she frequently gets questions from readers about her open-ended books. "Why don't you just finish them?" they ask. She replies:

> Hey, I stopped writing on page 296, so it's finished, okay? But no story can end just because I stopped writing. It goes soaring on, like our thoughts, still potent. Even if I killed off every major character, the way Shakespeare piled the bodies up in *Hamlet*. Life with a capital L would go on. Every "ending" is simply a compact between writer and reader to stop now, at a point of balance, at a moment when we both agree that the characters have gained enough strength, courage or insight to go on triumphantly without us. Personally, I keep expecting postcards from the people I've created and sent out into the world. ("Balancing the Books," 42)

Sebestyen feels that tying things up into a neat little package is too easy, and that it does not challenge the reader to think beyond the book. Most of us would agree that the best books are those we wonder about long after we have put them down: these are the books that make us question and speculate, the ones we choose to read again and again, hoping to gain more insight. Readers who become disappointed or upset over Sebestyen's open endings must realize that she is "making her magic" on them— even while they feel frustrated or angry. In laying bare our human weaknesses, she shows us how to forgive each other— and, above all, how to draw on our own inner strength in times of emotional need.

In spite of the critical acclaim she has received for her work, Sebestyen remains humble—to the point even of seeming self-deprecatory at times. "I'm not a fluent writer by nature," she says. "My body of work is still a ninety-pound weakling. . . . It took me a while to get the hang of it. I still plod along like a snail in molasses. And to my dismay, each new book is harder to write than the one before" ("Balancing the Books," 39).

Always a shy person, she never shared her early writings—not even with those closest to her—and she is still reluctant to discuss work in progress. In her early days as a writer she frequently used pseudonyms, penning short stories under the names of Lisa Dockery (her maiden name) and Joe Katy; and later on she even wrote under the name Igen Sebestyen. Like most writers, she practices "writing avoidance" whenever possible: "I get up at 6:00 A.M. and walk the dog, and do the chores, anything to keep from starting."

She laughs about the fact that she still writes in longhand, even though her son insists that she learn to use a word processor. "That's the next step," she says. "When I get settled, I'll learn to think that way." She adds:

> But I love to curl up in the sun, or in the shade of the trees, with my little scratch paper, and work that way. It's just like an artist, potter, or something. I like to feel it, but I know that's an archaic way to write now.

A good writer is, of course, an artist with words, and Sebestyen has always felt the desire to create. At one point, she wanted to be a designer, and she has always been interested in crafts, painting, and sculpting. "I didn't have anybody to teach me," she says, "and not much money to send me off someplace to learn." So she concentrated her attention on writing.

After several unsold adult novels and about fifty adult stories, she decided to try writing for a younger audience. Having made that decision, she set out to read as many books for young people as possible. The first writer of young adult books she came to respect is Lloyd Alexander: she admired him (and many other writers she later read) because they "tackled problems" and tried to foster in kids that sense that they are not alone—the knowledge that other people share the same problems.

Though she consciously made the decision to write for a younger audience, Sebestyen's books are not market-driven. She writes because she has something to say, not because romances or problem novels happen to be selling. Like all artists, her desire to create stems from a need to express a deeply felt idea or truth, to emphasize the universality of life's experiences. In fact, two of her novels, *Words by Heart* and *Far from Home*, have been described by some reviewers as transcending the boundaries between young adult and adult fiction. The family problems faced by her characters, the search for love and understanding, the struggle to find a place in the world are all dilemmas that know no particular age or time.

Concluding her speech at the Children's Literature Association conference, Sebestyen quotes a line from William Faulkner's Nobel Prize acceptance speech, in which he says,

> I believe that man will not merely endure, he will prevail. He is immortal, not because he alone among creatures has an inexhaustible voice, but because he has a soul, a spirit capable of compassion and sacrifice and endurance. The writer's duty is to write about these things. ("Balancing the Books," 44)

Sebestyen takes this duty seriously.

3. *Words by Heart*

> We will match your capacity to inflict suffering with our capacity to endure suffering. We will meet your physical force with soul force. We will not hate you, but we cannot in all good conscience obey your unjust laws. . . We will soon wear you down by our capacity to suffer. And in winning our freedom, we will so appeal to your heart and conscience that we will win you in the process.
>
> —Martin Luther King, Jr., August 1963

Among Ouida Sebestyen's materials is a slip of paper on which she has written the above quote from Dr. Martin Luther King, Jr. Discussing her novel *Words by Heart*, she mentions that King's ideas helped shape the book, even though the story takes place in the early 1900s. This is an interesting revelation, given the fact that several reviewers criticized the book as the antithesis of Dr. King's teachings.

Sebestyen's award-winning first novel tells the story of twelve-year-old Lena Sills, possessed of a "magic mind" that devours books and prizes learning. When Lena enters a Bible-quoting contest as the only black contestant pitted against several white students, her tenacity and determination to win result in a standoff with the town's top student, Winslow Starnes. But Lena's memorizing skills prove to be too much even for Winslow, and she becomes the undisputed champion. Her glorious moment is spoiled, however, when she sees that her prize is a blue bow tie, obviously meant for Winslow. Rejecting the prize, Lena is loathe to accept the fact that she was expected to lose.

Lena's father Ben had moved his family to the western town of Bethel Springs from an all-black settlement in the South called Scattercreek. Though they felt secure there, Ben wanted more for his family than the limited existence possible in the South. The country was expanding westward, and he felt that there was plenty of room for everyone to live and grow.

Unfortunately, jealousy and racial hatred exist in Bethel Springs, too, as Lena quickly learns when her father takes a job that a drunken white sharecropper, Henry Haney, has lost. Taunted by Haney and his eldest son, Tater, Lena's family suffers fear and humiliation. But Ben Sills refuses to protest or retaliate, believing instead in the Bible's injunctions to "turn the other cheek" and to "love thine enemy." Thus begins Lena's struggle between her natural inclination to rail against injustice, on the one hand, and her deep-seated desire to please and emulate her father, on the other.

The family's problems are compounded when their employer, the eccentric, unhappy Mrs. Chism, insists on using Ben as a model of good behavior, which further infuriates Henry Haney. Though she is often cruel in her remarks to Lena, Ben, and Lena's stepmother, Claudie, Ben reminds them that Mrs. Chism is their employer and that they must submit to her demands. As tenant farmers on her land, they are at the mercy of her whims, so Lena must sometimes miss her school classes to help Mrs. Chism with the housework.

It is during one of these cleaning sessions that Lena discovers a stack of old books in Mrs. Chism's attic, a find that excites her, since she loves to learn. When Mrs. Chism refuses to let her borrow the books, Lena smuggles one out in her bookbag, intending to return it as soon as she has read it. Later, when she borrows a second book and it is accidently destroyed by her little brother's spilled milk, Ben guesses her secret and insists she confess to Mrs. Chism. At first violently angry, Mrs. Chism eventually strikes a bargain with Ben: she'll let Lena borrow her books if he'll take the wagon and go over to mend the fences at Hawk Hill—a job Henry Haney has always done in the past, and one that will require Ben to be away from home for a few days.

At this point, the novel moves toward its climax, as Ben tells Lena he wants her to be Claudie's "right-hand man" while he is gone. All this time, Lena has gradually been coming to realize just how much her father loves her—something for which she always craved reassurance. When Ben doesn't return from Hawk Hill by the appointed time, Lena sets out alone and on foot to find him, afraid he has come to harm. The darkness and unfamiliar ground do not deter her. "She had never gone anywhere in the night before. Maybe that was lucky. She didn't know what to be scared of."[1] Her worst suspicions are realized, however, when she finds her bleeding father drawing his last breaths and his assailant, Tater Haney, badly injured. Her devotion to her father is put to the test as he instructs her, in his final moments, to help Tater first, since he has a chance to live. Lena is torn apart at the thought of saving her father's killer, realizing that God's words are easy to memorize but hard to live by. As she helps Tater into the wagon, she is comforted by the thought that Ben will continue to live through her.

A portion of *Words by Heart* first appeared as a short story in *Ingenue* in December of 1968. Sebestyen later submitted the story to the publishing company Little, Brown in January 1978, asking Melanie Kroupa, then a children's book editor there, if she saw any promise in it. Kroupa replied that if Sebestyen would like to expand the story into a novel, she would be glad to look at it. The author was so encouraged that she finished the book in three months.[2]

Though the story is fictional, Sebestyen based it on her own experiences growing up in the small town of Vernon, Texas. In fact, it was her aunt who inspired the character of Lena. "She took care of seven kids; saw them all through college and provided a very strong foundation," says the author. The Bible-quoting contest in which Lena competes is also drawn from an experience Sebestyen's aunt had as a young girl—right down to the prize of the blue bow-tie. Another coincidence lies in the fact that Lena Sills was born the same year as Sebestyen's mother, 1898. "[W]hen I was uncertain about school lunches or girls wearing black stockings back in 1910," says Sebestyen, "I just yelled into the kitchen and she'd yell back answers" (Mercier, 40).

Central Themes and Problems

The center of *Words by Heart* is really the father-daughter relationship between Ben and Lena Sills, reminiscent in some ways
of the relationship between Sebestyen and her own father, who
died not long before she wrote the novel. Lena's desire to impress
her father is apparent in the very first chapter, when we learn
that Lena had begun memorizing Bible verses when she learned
from Claudie that her father had once hoped to be a preacher, "as
if that were something she could do to make it up to Papa"
(*Heart*, 9). She chose the verses her father liked, but she kept
other verses close to her heart—verses from the Song of
Solomon, which no one knew she had memorized. Summoning
the words that waited at the back of her mind, Lena recites,

> I am black, but comely,
> O ye daughters of Jerusalem,
> As the tents of Kedar,
> As the curtains of Solomon.
> . . . I am the rose of
> Sharon, and the lily
> of the valleys— (*Heart*, 12)

The words transform Lena, as she sees herself "beautiful, thin as
a flower, blooming with the hope of love" (*Heart*, 12). But she
worries about revealing her dreams to a roomful of people as she
recites verse after verse of the Song. Later, after winning the contest, she worries about making Papa sad, "saying the Song of
Solomon like that, revealing before all those strangers that her
life lacked something" (*Heart*, 16). Confused by her longing for a
better life, Lena feels guilty and frustrated. Added to the embarrassment of winning a boy's prize is the fear that she has hurt
her beloved father. On the ride home, as Ben reminds her that
being "somebody" comes from inside, not from winning a prize,
Lena thinks, "But it was for you. . . . You were the only prize I
really wanted. You proud of me" (*Heart*, 17).

Lena's devotion to her father is understandable. Her mother
died when she was three, and she and Ben had only each other

until he married Claudie, two years later. And though she gets along well with Claudie and takes care of her stepbrothers and stepsister, Lena needs desperately to fill the void left by her mother's death. One morning, watching the youngest children, Roy and Armilla, sleeping, Lena wonders if the fact that they look like their mother is due to her being there for them to "copy somehow"—and if that is so, then how will she ever know who to be? (*Heart*, 23).

This question strikes at the heart of Lena's problem throughout the book. It might be argued that her close identification with her father results in her being silenced as a young woman, a consequence lamented by more than one critic of *Words by Heart*. "The most puzzling and distressing aspect of Lena's character is that she begins as a proud fighter and ends as a model of meek Christian forbearance, exactly . . . like her saintly father," writes Kristin Hunter in *The Washington Post*.[3] George Ford, illustrator of *Paul Robeson* and other children's books writes:

> The author of *Words by Heart* may have intended a tribute to the human spirit. What she actually does is mindlessly celebrate the gradual disintegration of a spirit. One feels that Lena will forsake her drive for success—not because she is weak, but because she is Black.[4]

It is questionable whether Lena's "disintegration of spirit" actually takes place, and, if so, whether it is due entirely to her color. After all, a child of any race might be so influenced by blind devotion to a saintly father. But it is certain that she does change from a feisty, questioning young woman to a calmer, more accepting person by the end of the book. Psychologists such as Carol Gilligan might see this as another example of a female adolescent's voice being silenced by compliance to the wishes of an authoritarian male. Gilligan studied adolescent girls at the Emma Willard School in Troy, N.Y., where she found "that the time between ages eleven and sixteen is an especially critical one in girls' lives and that the crisis is one of relationship."[5] One researcher in Gilligan's study, Jamie Victoria Ward, spent time interviewing a group of young minority women there; in her findings, she cites the theories of the psychiatrist Erik Erikson on how important the development of identity is in adolescents, and she points out that "the integration of the individual's personal identity with [his or her] racial identity is a necessary and inevitable developmental task of growing up black in white America" (Gilligan et al., 218). Ward notes that the negative images about race that are transmitted to black children often cause them to think of themselves as inferior. To prevent this from happening, she asserts that black adolescents must say, "I am not what you believe black people to be, *and I am black*" (Gilligan et al., 219).

If we think about Lena Sills in this light, we can see that she is certainly seeking identity: for example, she wonders who she will become, since she has no female role model in her life with whom she strongly identifies. Also, she and her family have been treated poorly because of their race. Mrs. Chism, for example, can't imagine why Lena would want to read books. "What good do you think books would do you?" she asks sarcastically (*Heart*, 43). And Henry Haney, when Ben offers him a ride in his wagon, replies venomously, "I don't have to ride with Sambos" (*Heart*, 69). Through all of this, however, Lena maintains her pride; she even becomes more determined to "be somebody" someday. She is not cowed by Mrs. Chism's mean-spirited remarks, nor is she intimidated by Henry Haney's racist anger. The problem for some readers seems to be that Lena shows strong evidence of moving toward identity achievement, only to become confused by her father's passive submissiveness. Since he is the role model she identifies closely with, she tends to think of her own behavior as always wrong and his as the standard to be achieved. After being scolded by her father for coming to his defense when Tater shoves the barn door in his face, Lena is miserable:

> She could never be like Papa, forgetting herself as he forgot himself. It seemed that he stood at a distance, seeing that everything was very small inside immense space, seeing that events

were blinks of time in endless time, not important enough to
hurt him or scare him. She couldn't do it. (*Heart*, 75)

It is only through Ben's death at the end of the book that Lena
realizes who she wants to be. Although some readers have found
her choice to be troubling, we need not give up on her. True, she
wonders what will fill the empty space left by Ben; but Sebestyen
does not imply that Lena will wait passively for life to come to
her. It is clear that Lena still eagerly awaits the future, and she
still has her aspirations.

Generally, *Words by Heart* was received very well. Impressed
by Lena's character and by the book as a whole, the poet Nikki
Giovanni writes:

> Lena is the kind of smart, sensitive, bold little girl we all wish
> we had been. *Words by Heart* is a marvelous memoir of child-
> hood that spans the distance between what we feel and what
> we say.[6]

Writing in *English Journal*, James Brewbaker points out that
Words by Heart is "an account of religious values in action," one
that dramatizes the gap between superficial beliefs and those
which have truly been learned "by heart."[7]

Though most reviews of *Words by Heart* were positive, some
critics questioned the ability of a white author to write with
authority about the black experience. Rudine Sims, for example,
believes the book "is flawed because it presents an outsider's perspective on Black lives and fails to recognize the political, racial
and social realities that shape the Black Experience in this country" (Sims, 12). In arguing this point, she cites especially Ben
Sill's "turn the other cheek" behavior:

> The cumulative picture of Ben Sills is the prototype of the "good
> Negro"—hard working, Bible-quoting, understanding, passive,
> loving and forgiving towards whites, and willing to "wait on the
> Lord" until whites are ready to accept his family. . . . Sills lives

> to serve others—and those others (outside of his family) are
> white. (Sims, 14)

Sims criticizes Sebestyen's justification of Ben's passivity,
which appears to be connected to his former desire to be a
preacher, saying "it is false to equate godliness with passivity."
As evidence, she points out that "Dr. Martin Luther King, Jr.
was non-violent, but not passive" (Sims, 14). Likewise, Kristin
Hunter, writing in the *Washington Post* asserts, "If Sebestyen's
brand of meek, turn-the-other-cheek Christianity is supposed to
fill the voids left by Malcolm [X] and, yes, Martin, then we blacks
and our youngsters will be in even deeper trouble" (Hunter, E3).
Discussing the theology of the book, Fay Wilson-Beach and
Glyger G. Beach lament that:

> *Words by Heart* does not use scripture to encourage change. The
> book quotes scripture that would have people give control of
> their lives to a benign God; it blatantly ignores scriptural admo-
> nitions that would support people taking responsible actions in
> their own affairs as well as those of their neighbors.[8]

They also regret that "Ben Sills's death does not stir [the] community to any redemptive acts. After Ben's murder, the white
characters indulge in post mortem trivia" (Beach and Beach, 17).
Like Sims, they charge that the kind of "passive love" in *Words
by Heart* is not the sort of love preached by Martin Luther King,
Jr. "*Words by Heart* is not a book for Black children but for white
racists," say the Beaches (Beach and Beach, 17).

Rather than being offended by these negative reviews, Sebestyen feels that she can learn from them. "I know it's a sensitive
thing for people who have had to deal with this all their lives," she
says:

> I didn't worry about it as I was writing because it didn't occur
> to me that I was doing anything unusual. . . . I wasn't thinking
> in terms of my character being black and my being white. . . . I
> grew up in Texas with the Ku Klux Klan around, so the book
> was partly an apology, I guess, for my earlier lack of awareness.

. . . I wanted to say something about how brave they were and how hard it must have been.

About the character of Ben, Sebestyen says:

> I can see that from a black point of view, yes, he's very Uncle Tom-ish. It's just that he was a very special and wonderful person—too good—and when you write about somebody too good, it doesn't seem natural, it doesn't seem real. . . . I thought of him as almost a biblical figure, the ideal father. . . . It didn't occur to me that his being black would turn him into [a stereotype] . . . But when you read the journals or notes from that period, the post–Civil War time, the people writing them just knock you out with their sensitivity, this unabashed goodness they had. . . . It was just that Ben had sort of stepped up on another plane beyond most of us, but it's hard to explain that to anyone whose main focus is on race.

Sebestyen feels that we read fiction because we need to see heroes who are bigger than life. It is rare to find such people in the real world, but that part of us that strives for perfection needs to be reminded of what we can be, what we are capable of. For her, Ben Sills is that reminder.

The criticism based on racial issues that has been leveled at *Words by Heart* and other young adult novels by the Council on Interracial Books for Children (CIBC), through their *Interracial Books for Children Bulletin*, has caught the attention of some experts in the field. In *Literature for Today's Young Adults*, Ken Donelson and Allen Pace Nilsen describe this criticism as "a call for censorship based on social awareness."[9] Though they certainly agree with the CIBC's goals—to promote literature that reflects the multiracial society in which we live—they question how terms such as "racist" and "sexist" are used to replace discussions of literary merit. Donelson and Nilsen feel that such negative reviews based solely on subjective personal judgements from an influential organization like CIBC may dissuade librarians from stocking many worthy books and teachers from using the books in their classrooms. As an example of such thinking, they cite a 1976 article by Bettye I. Latimer that appeared in *The*

Reading Teacher, in which the author suggests that all "racist-oriented" books be placed in the library's archives. "All censors," say Donelson and Nilsen, "whatever their religious or sociological biases, *know* what is good and bad in books and are only too willing to *help* the rest of us fumbling mortals learn what to keep and what to exile (or put in the archives)" (Donelson and Nilsen, 435).

While it is impossible to know how many teachers and librarians were affected by reviews describing *Words by Heart* as racist, letters to the author from readers indicate overwhelming acceptance. In addition, the novel received a long list of awards: it was a *New York Times* Best Book and a *School Library Journal* Best Book; it was listed as one of *Learning Magazine*'s Ten Best Books of the Year, the American Library Association's (ALA) Notable Children's Books, the ALA's Best Books for Young Adults, and the Library of Congress's Children's Book of the Year; and it received the International Reading Association Children's Book Award. *Reader's Digest* even published an illustrated, condensed version, which is notable for a book marketed for young readers. The Public Broadcasting System also broadcast a film version for its *Wonderworks* series on February 11, 1985. Fran Robinson starred in the role of Lena with Robert Hooks and Alfre Woodard as Ben and Claudie. Though the movie loses some of the novel's depth, it does capture the significance of the relationship between Lena and Ben, as well as the struggle with which Lena must contend.

Perhaps the strongest reason that *Words by Heart* has been so widely acclaimed is that it presents universal themes, the most significant of which is the striving for perfection. This is evident on a simple level in Lena's desire to be "somebody," to be the best at something. She is fiercely determined to win the scripture-quoting contest and refuses to settle for tying with Winslow Starnes. She hungers to read books and newspapers, so much so that she even disregards what she has learned about right and wrong behavior when she "borrows" Mrs. Chism's books to satisfy her craving. She even competes for the attention of Winslow Starnes against the white girl, Elsie Rawley—not so much to win Winslow's affection as to revel in the competition itself, and to satisfy her craving for thoughtful discussion about books and poetry. When Winslow chooses her company over Elsie's, Lena is wary at first; gradually, though, she comes to trust him. When Winslow compliments her on being good at memorizing, "a compliment he had carried long enough" Sebestyen tells us,

> The flush kept spreading along her arms, the way springtime sap must move through a tree. She expected to see little green leaves sprouting from her fingertips. . . . Maybe leaf buds were opening in her hair. Maybe her mouth was unfolding into a flower. (*Heart*, 93)

Lena blooms in Winslow's warmth as she never has bloomed before, in a scene symbolic of the growth taking place within her throughout the book; this growth is foreshadowed early on, when she recites a passage from the Song of Solomon. Even as she strives for the perfection her father represents to her, she achieves her own kind of perfection as a twelve-year-old on the brink of becoming a young woman. By the end of the book, she knows that she is "somebody" *already*, and that she will continue her quest to be "the best." She will remember her father's wish— "I want you not to know your place" (*Heart*, 106)—as she makes her way through life without him.

As a twelve-year-old who is beginning to experience the emotional pain and insecurity of adolescence, Lena strives to be the best in order to impress others, especially her father. Ben, on the other hand, seeks perfection of the self through the spirit: "When you're somebody inside yourself," he tells Lena, "you don't need to be told" (*Heart*, 17). When Lena asks him if it's wrong to want to be better than other people, he tells her, "the thing you want to strive for, always, is to be better than yourself. And we all fall short on that" (*Heart*, 22). A true pacifist, Ben believes that violence and killing are wrong under any circumstances, and his refusal to fight back against threats and taunts is a continual source of frustration to Lena. Sebestyen foreshadows Ben's death more than once; it seems clear at one point that Ben is aware he may not have long to live. Talking about the mountains, which he has never seen, he tells his family, "If I don't get to see them, you all can see them for me" (*Heart*, 50). When Lena becomes visibly upset at this remark, Ben simply gazes at her with a fading smile. His sense of impending death does not prevent him from making the three-day ride to Hawk Hill to mend Mrs. Chism's fences, even though he has been threatened by the Haneys. When he is fatally shot by Tater, he almost embraces death, using his rapidly dwindling strength to help his attacker rather than trying to save himself. Unable to comprehend the injustice of the situation, Lena asks Ben, "Why was it you and not him, Papa? Where was the shield and buckler of the Lord?" "I don't know, Lena," he replies. "I wrestled all night with that, and you'll have to wrestle too, til you get an answer. There's an answer" (*Heart*, 144). Reminding Lena that he will continue to live through her, he sends her off to find the horse, so she won't have to watch him die. Ben appears, "too good to be true" to some readers, but perhaps he is just too good for this life. Certainly, Sebestyen intended to portray him in this way. His striving for spiritual perfection, though difficult to rationalize at times, creates a powerful theme that—along with Lena's quest for self-actualization—is perhaps better understood with the heart than with the mind.

Secondary Themes

A second theme that permeates *Words by Heart* is that of death and rebirth. When the Sills' dog, Bullet, is found dead, most likely poisoned by the Haneys, Lena becomes angry and wishes for revenge. Soon after, the family cat gives birth to kittens, and Ben tells Lena, "Something always comes to fill the empty places. . . . Something comes to take the place of what you lose" (*Heart*, 37). When Lena thinks back, she realizes that his words have held true for her: after her mother died, she was cared for by a succession of relatives while Ben was at work, but he found Claudie, who helped to fill the emptiness in their lives. Soon after that, Ben and Claudie had children, and Lena was no longer an only child.

The most significant manifestation of this theme, however, occurs when Ben is killed, and Lena must cope with the knowledge that she has lost the person most dear to her. Ben's death occurs in late fall, when all of nature seems to be dying. But like the buds that will surely sprout in the spring, we know that Lena will emerge from her grief a stronger person, seasoned already by cruelty and loss, but more determined than ever to make the most of life. Only through Ben's death could Lena be reborn—a new Lena, who embodies the best of her father *and* the best of herself.

The theme of family, of course, is strong throughout the book, especially in the father-daughter relationship between Lena and Ben. At the beginning of the novel, Lena acknowledges how much she needs her father, even though she is old enough to be less dependent on him. Later on in the story, however, she muses on the slow change in their relationship: remembering the "juicy kisses" she used to give him when she was small, she regrets that she can no longer show this kind of affection, for fear of clinging to Ben when she ought to be breaking away.

Lena is often confused about her feelings toward Ben. At the scripture-quoting contest, she becomes embarrassed about his appearance, wishing he had bathed and washed away the cotton-gin dust on his clothes and face. Later in the story, when she is especially angry at his refusal to stand up to the Haneys, she wonders what he would do if someone tried to hurt his family. When Claudie tells her that Ben struggles with this worry every day, Lena is aghast. This helps to explain why he waits to walk her home when she leaves Mrs. Chism's at dusk. Though Lena is grateful, she is also puzzled, since this behavior seems uncharacteristic of Ben.

The beginning of the change in their relationship is marked by an interesting passage, when Ben takes Lena for a walk to tell her about their dog Bullet's death. At first, Lena "stumbled along behind him" and "his back was like a stranger's" as he talks of the racial injustice he had seen (*Heart*, 30). When he shows her Bullet's grave, and she begins to blame Tater Haney, her father's stern look stops her in mid-sentence. Her anger at her father surprises her, and she turns away to walk back home. This time, though, it is Ben who follows behind in silence. Part of Lena wishes he would touch her and comfort her, but another part knows that she would shrug off his attempt to console her.

This incident, however small, symbolizes Lena's quest for independence, her wish to pull away from her father. Even as she feels confused by her feelings of love and anger, she is moving slowly toward the independence she seeks.

Lena does not love Ben any less; rather, she begins to love him differently—as a friend and protector rather than a clinging child. She springs to his defense when Tater Haney slams the barn door into Ben's face, walloping Tater with her bookbag, which contains Mrs. Chism's *Pearls from the American Poets*. Though Lena fears for Ben's safety, they later laugh about the incident, with Papa calling her "my avenging angel" (*Heart*, 74). "Now Tater's had a bellyful of the American poets," he jokes, as they collapse into conspiratorial laughter (*Heart*, 77).

The role reversal becomes complete when Lena makes the decision to travel alone, on foot, across unfamiliar ground to find her father. Fighting off hunger and fatigue, she follows his wagon tracks, marching on toward the medicine hills "crouched like giants, daring her to pass between them. . . . scowling through black cedar beards" (*Heart*, 136). Pushing negative thoughts out of her mind, she travels on until she finds her father, mortally wounded, in need of her help. Now Lena is the protector, the decision-maker. Now *she* must struggle with the question Ben wrestled with every day: What will I do if someone tries to hurt my family? As their relationship comes full circle, Lena makes the decision: she will be merciful to her father's killer. She will carry on her father's legacy. But we get the feeling she will do it in her own way.

Significance of Minor Characters

A discussion of *Words by Heart* would not be complete without some attention to its minor characters. Claudie, for example, plays an important role in Lena's growth. Unlike Ben, she resents the racial discrimination she has experienced, and she is not at all convinced that moving west will make things better. She recalls with fear the nightriders who terrorized her neighbors and family when she was a girl, telling Lena, "It's like a blight. . . . You know it's going to spread till it kills off what was growing so good." (*Heart*, 127)

It is Claudie who keeps insisting that Ben tell Lena how life really is for black people, but it is also Claudie who scolds Lena for questioning her father's refusal to fight back. Though Claudie is fifteen years younger than Ben, Lena realizes how much her stepmother loves her father. When she witnesses a tender moment between them as they prepare for bed one night, she sees that Claudie is crying in her father's arms. She begins to suspect that Claudie's rather tough exterior masks fears about which Lena knows little.

By the end of the novel, it seems that Lena may have a role model after all. Claudie decides to stay in Bethel Springs because it was Ben's hope for their future. Standing up to Mrs. Chism and the other white townspeople, she announces proudly that she and her children will carry on Ben's legacy, noting that her two sons will "be the same threat . . . that Ben was" (*Heart*, 160).

Winslow Starnes, too, has a positive effect on Lena. Though some critics have charged that he is the stereotypical "good white person" in the story, his attempts to befriend Lena and her family—against his father's wishes—help Lena to see that people must assess each other as individuals, not by their color or community standing. Lena blossoms in his presence because he sees her as an equal. He needs her as much as she needs him—to share a love of books and poetry, to learn that color disappears in the face of friendship.

Even Mrs. Chism contributes to Lena's emotional growth in the novel. Though she is a demanding, cantankerous old woman, Lena eventually realizes that Mrs. Chism's crankiness stems from the fact that she is lonely and unhappy. When she throws a huge dinner party and only Jaybird Kelsey attends, Lena feels sorry for her and goes over to cheer her up. And though Mrs.

Chism accuses her of wanting the leftover food, and ends up throwing a potted fern at the portrait of her dead husband, Lena stays to clean up the mess when Mrs. Chism flees to her room. Lena, her compassion aroused, realizes that Mrs. Chism also wants to be somebody, but that wealth is no guarantee of success.

Finally, the Haney family figures strongly in Lena's character development. As a foil to Ben, Henry Haney seems to lack self-esteem and purpose. But Lena notices his proud bearing as he mounts his horse, and she pictures the young man who, in his cowbow days, was the best at what he did. She feels sad at what has been lost and wonders why they cannot all just get along and be friends. At one point she remembers Ben telling her that the Haneys are much worse off than her own family is: her family rents their land, whereas the Haneys are merely sharecroppers. At the end of the novel, when Lena sees Haney picking their cotton for them, she hopes that he is trying to make amends, though she suspects that he might be trying to get them to keep silent about Tater's crime. And Tater himself is a source of consternation to Lena. Though she has professed hatred for him and his family, she finds herself noticing his delicate long fingers as she helps load his injured body into the wagon. "Not a farmer's hand," she thinks, remembering "the little windmill at the corner of the Haney's brush arbor that he must have made" (*Heart*, 147–148). The fact that she can think these thoughts, under the circumstances, is evidence that she has matured. The Haneys are a vehicle through which these changes in Lena become apparent.

Looking again at the words of Martin Luther King, Jr., it appears that Ouida Sebestyen has, indeed, created a novel that combats hatred with love, that champions freedom through suffering. But perhaps that love and freedom are not of this world, and therein lies the source of contention.

4. *Far from Home*

GO TO TOM BUCKLEY HE TAKE YOU IN LOVE HIM. The orders were clear. Salty's job was to obey them, to find work and a home for himself and his eighty-four-year-old great-grandmother, Mam. His mother had written the note in "rickety child-letters" as she lay dying in the hospital, hopeful that Salty and Mam would find security—and maybe even love—at the home of Tom Buckley. But why should Buckley agree to take them in? And why on earth should Salty be expected to love a man he doesn't even know?

Thirteen-year-old Salty Yeager struggled with these questions for months. He was proud and wanted to be independent, but the reality was that he and Mam would starve if he did not find a job to support them. When he wakes up one June morning to a breakfast of two and a half crackers and "all the water he could hold, to fool his stomach into thinking he had fed it,"[1] he makes his decision: he will humble himself and go to the Buckley Arms boarding house in order to ask for a job and living quarters for Mam and himself. His mother had worked for the Buckleys fifteen years, so he feels his chances are good. As Salty makes his way to the rooming house, he remembers his beloved mother, the mute Dovie who hadn't spoken a word since being locked in a trunk by her father when she was a little girl. Though silent, she had always managed to communicate her love to Salty, who grieved sorely at her death. He had made a promise to her, and he would keep it. Tom Buckley just had to take them in.

But Tom is reluctant—even hostile—when Salty appears at his door. Even though his wife, Babe, welcomes Salty with open arms

when she learns he is Dovie's son, Tom resists committing himself. He is not doing well financially, and he is obviously uncomfortable with the thought of having Salty around. However, at
Babe's continued urging, Tom relents and agrees to a temporary
arrangement. He makes it plain that he plans to sell the boarding
house if business does not improve. Tom gets even more than he
bargained for when he discovers that Salty's pet gander,
Tollybosky, is also part of the deal.

Salty's experience at the Buckley Arms that summer is a mixture of pleasure and pain. He has fun with Babe's nephew, Hardy
McCaslin, a hilarious practical joker, but he senses serious trouble between Hardy and his wife, Rose Ann. He develops a filial
attachment to Jo Miller, a pregnant woman he discovers wandering the streets, but finds his need for her emotional support troubling. He appreciates Babe's delicious cooking and her kindness
to him, but he resents her hold on Tom Buckley. And he struggles constantly with his feelings for Tom—the man he suspects
may be his father. Tom's failure or refusal to acknowledge him is
a wound too deep for a thirteen-year-old to bear. Throughout the
novel, the two of them dance around each other cautiously, like
boxers in a ring. Tom tries in his own way to show that he cares,
but he fears hurting Babe, should she ever learn the truth. Salty
needs Tom's love and approval, but his anger and naïveté keep
him from understanding Tom's predicament.

Added to Salty's woes is the pesky little girl across the street,
Idalee Eversole. She and her siblings frequently suffer abuse at
the hands of their father, and it is most likely from him that she
learned the word "bastard"—an epithet she hurls at Salty one
day when Tom is within earshot. Though Idalee's curiosity and
persistence prove to be an annoyance to Salty, it is clear that she
genuinely likes him and wants to be his friend. In fact, it is
through Idalee that he begins to understand that liking someone
is a risk you take just because you want to.

The novel's climax occurs on the Fourth of July—a fitting time
for new beginnings—when a series of incidents helps Salty to
bring his future into focus. He begins to realize that Mam cannot
live forever and that he will be ready to deal with her death when

the time comes. He knows that Tom loves him, and he begins to understand that he will have to settle for a private declaration of that love. As he waves his Fourth of July sparkler in a giant circle and writes his name in light, Salty's search for a home has ended, but his search for an identity is just beginning.

Originally entitled *Dovie's Boy* in early drafts, *Far from Home* is Ouida Sebestyen's favorite of her own books. "I don't know why," she says, "except that often when you get a wonderful idea for a book and write it, it's never that wonderful idea. . . . It becomes something else. But this one stayed nearest to the original idea." Thinking about what she set out to do in this book, she muses:

> I think I tried to see if I could handle more characters than the first book. It was something I wanted to try. I wanted to try to handle more themes and more conflicts and see if I had more things to say. . . . Whatever it was that I felt the need to write about, I seem to have done it because at the end I said, "Yeah, good."

Sebestyen patterned the character of Mam after her own mother, "the essence of a wonderful woman." Her mother died the day after she finished *Far from Home*, and she marvels now at the fact that she could have continued writing during such a difficult time, when she knew her mother was dying. "I haven't read it since it first came out," she says, implying that the book evokes memories that are too painful.

Several critics who reviewed *Far from Home* commented that the book focuses as much on the adults in the story as it does on Salty's dilemma. For example, a review in *Horn Book* points out that "Even though Salty's constant but frustrated attempts to communicate with his father are presented in skillfully under-stated terms, an excessive proportion of the narrative is focused on the marital problems of the adults living in the boarding-house."[2] Similarly, *Booklist* agrees that "some of the concerns seem more adult than child-oriented."[3] Though *Far from Home* is definitely Salty's story, the adults do indeed play prominent roles; but this a strength of the book rather than a weakness. At a time when far too many young adult novels are criticized as being of interest only to adolescents, Ouida Sebestyen has given us a book that speaks to all generations. Even though Salty does not fully understand the problems that the adults are experiencing, their lives do touch his in ways that encourage his growth throughout the novel. Tom's loyalty to and love for Babe, her willingness to forgive his imperfections, Rose Ann's leaving and Hardy's painful confrontation of his childlike self, and Jo's desire to give her husband a second chance in spite of his past mistakes—these are examples through which Salty learns what loving really means. Sometimes it hurts, and sometimes it feels good—but always it is a risk.

In discussing *Far from Home*, it is very important to note that several of the characters appear in an early draft of a novel for adults that Sebestyen began to write in January 1968. Untitled and unfinished, the story focused on several adults living in Tom and Inez Buckley's boarding house in the late 1960s. Among the characters are the Buckleys, the McCaslins, Jo Shanewise (an early version of Jo Miller), whose estranged husband compelled her to have an abortion, and an old black woman named Majesta Chism, who had the gift of second sight (and who, incidentally, wore her cane tied to her waist, as Mam does in *Far from Home*). Sebestyen is not sure why she never finished the novel, but she speculates that these characters remained in her mind over the years and resurfaced when she felt the need to tell Salty's story.

Major Themes

Several prominent themes emerge from *Far from Home*, interwoven so tightly that the individual threads are barely discernible. The motifs of love, responsibility, birth, and identity permeate the novel, and each of these themes can be explored through the relationships of the various characters. In the very first chapter, Sebestyen establishes the close bond between Salty and his greatgrandmother, as Salty saves her two and a half of the five crackers left for breakfast, and she remarks, "I wish to goodness I could be a help, instead of trouble. You ought not to be loaded down with burdens bigger than you are" (*Home*, 5). Salty's assurance that she is no burden doesn't fool her a bit, but he is all that she has, and they need each other. Salty is fiercely protective of Mam, feeling entirely responsible for her well-being. Though he tires of her repeated reminiscences, he listens politely and will not allow others to criticize her. When he overhears Babe complaining to Tom that Mam is a nuisance, he becomes angry and develops mixed feelings toward the otherwise kindly Babe. Near the end of the novel, when Mam wanders away from home, and he and Tom set out to find her, Salty, fearing that she may have come to harm, searches frantically. Feeling compelled to continue the search, lest they stop just short of finding her, he feels guilty because "she had prayed for him so much, and he didn't know what to say for her" (*Home*, 182–183).

A different kind of love is apparent in the relationship between Tom and Babe, a marital love based on loyalty and trust. Tom's failure to acknowledge Salty stems from the guilt he feels at having betrayed his wife by having an affair with Dovie, even though he and Babe were separated at the time. In trying to keep his emotional distance from Salty, he feels he is being loyal to his wife, who he believes has first claim on his love. Because they are unable to have children of their own (Babe has had several miscarriages), Tom wants to protect her from further hurt. At one point, when Hardy McCaslin makes a thoughtless comment about their childlessness, and Babe's face clouds over, Tom replies, "One baby is all I need. . . . One Babe" (*Home*, 54). Sebestyen described the character she set out to create in Babe this way:

> I wanted her to be different enough that Salty would differentiate between her and some ordinary woman. I wanted Salty to wonder why she could create such a sense of loyalty in Tom. Then gradually he began to understand her—maybe even to see that, to her, children were symbols of love or affection. Toward the end he began to see that part of her physical situation was that nobody fed her; she had to feed herself because something

was missing in her life. I wanted her to be almost like a baby . . . fat and sweet and innocent.

When Tom declares that Babe loves people by feeding them, Salty begins to realize that there are many ways to show love. Babe also shows her love for Tom by protecting him. Because he was exposed to poisonous gas in World War I and was stricken with pneumonia, he has a terrible lingering cough that worries Babe, and she is always seeking ways to lighten his workload. Though he is gruff and seemingly hard-hearted at times, she forgives him and tries to help others to see his goodness. A difficult and telling scene occurs early in the story when Babe is trying to convince Tom to take Salty in:

> Without warning, Tom's big-knuckled hand swung out and rapped her across the cheek. . . . "Oh, Lord," Tom said. Salty watched the hard edges of his mouth melt away until he was someone else. His different voice said, "Babe, you know I never did that before in my life. Babe. I don't know what happened. . . . Sweetheart, I'm just so tired . . . and now I'm taking it out on you." His hands fumbled to take hers and draw her back into the moment before he hit her. To Salty in the corner they seemed to be dancing to two different songs. "Babe, please," Tom begged. . . . you mean the world to me."
> "I know that," she said. "I know I do."
> With great dignity she let him touch her. (*Home*, 16)

In witnessing this scene, Salty discovers a tender side to Tom, a side that surfaces several times in the story when Tom lets his guard down.

Though the love between Tom and Babe is solidly grounded, the emotions surrounding the marriage of Hardy and Rose Ann McCaslin are transient and mercurial. Though he obviously adores her, she cannot come to terms with his aimlessness and cavalier attitude toward life. Like Tom, Hardy has a warm and caring side, but his childish pranks and embarrassing jokes outweigh these qualities for Rose Ann, who is frustrated by his irresponsibility and failure to hold a job. Her desperate attempt to keep their marriage together by becoming pregnant has an ironic opposite effect, when Hardy is angered by the news. Unlike Tom and Babe, Hardy and Rose Ann communicate very little, which puts stress on their marriage and pushes them further apart. When she feels it necessary to leave for a while to visit her sister, he can't understand her need for space and time to think. Convinced that Hardy does not want the baby, which Salty refers to fondly as "the bean," Rose Ann aborts the child, harming herself in the process. Sebestyen lets us know all this through Salty's observations, feeding us bits and pieces in the dialogue between Tom and Hardy. As Tom tries to help Hardy understand why Rose Ann had the abortion and what it took to make such a decision, Hardy declares that he had intended to love the unborn child. His declaration is not lost on the reader, for in some ways it parallels the situation between Tom and Dovie years before.

It is only through Rose Ann's desperate action that Hardy finally begins to realize that he has failed to take responsibility for his wife and his unborn child. His decision to leave in order to be with Rose Ann is a major step toward a new beginning for the two of them, and though Salty fears Hardy's leaving, he senses the power of his strengthening love for Rose Ann.

While Salty for the most part merely observes the events that take place between Hardy and Rose Ann, he is very much a participant in the events surrounding Jo Miller. At first he is actually her savior, as he discovers her wandering the streets alone, nine months pregnant without food or money. When she collapses and ends up staying at the Buckley Arms, Salty feels the need to watch over her, as though he is responsible for her welfare. When she eventually ends up having her baby in Salty's bed, with Salty on the other side of the door marveling at the miracle he hears, he begins to feel a closeness to Jo, a bond that continues to grow as she stays on at the boardinghouse. Jo becomes a mother figure to Salty, so much so that he becomes possessive of her and the baby. Rose Ann once had a dream that "the child from this house will change the world" (*Home*, 74), and though she and Hardy were thinking of their own baby when they described the dream, Salty is convinced that it is Jo's child who will make history. Salty believes that Jo's husband, a bootlegger, does not care about his wife or his child, and it makes him angry; confusing her situation with his own ambiguous relationship with Tom, Salty urges Jo not to tell her husband about the baby. He wants Jo to hate her husband, as he is trying to hate Tom.

Salty feels so bitter toward Tom that he is unable to separate his own life from Jo's. Hardy had once told him that his mother was very special because she saw the good in everybody. When Jo tells Salty that he is a loving person and asks him for advice, Salty senses a similarity between Jo's character and his mother's. When he questions Jo about her child changing the world, she replies, "Oh, Salty. We all change the world, don't we, by taking up space in it a little while, and touching each other's lives?" (*Home*, 123). Realizing that she is right, Salty is drawn to her: he begs her to stay on, because he needs her and because she is the only one, except for Mam, who sees the goodness in him.

When Jo decides to return to her husband, because she feels it is the responsible thing to do, Salty is devastated. He is still resentful even as he accompanies her to the train station. When she tries to hug him good-bye, he at first resists, then awkwardly returns her hug, still trying to convince her not to leave. Patiently Jo explains, "People have to work out their lives in their own way." But with her good-bye comes hope: she tells him, "I believe in you, Salty. . . . I don't turn loose of the people I love" (*Home*, 163). And so Jo leaves him, as Dovie did; but Salty is a little wiser now and on his way to a better understanding of the world and his place in it.

Salty's Development

Much of Salty's increased understanding comes about painfully as a result of his relationship with Tom Buckley. When Salty first arrives at the boardinghouse, it is plain that Tom is not happy to see him; thus, their relationship starts out on a hostile note. Salty is especially resentful when Tom tosses Dovie's "rickety child-letter" note out the car window, after insinuating that, given her inability to speak, anybody could have taken advantage of her and fathered Salty. (Interestingly, Sebestyen doesn't try to reconcile this insulting remark for the reader by showing a discomfort in Tom at making such an innuendo about a woman he respected—and briefly loved. It seems a bit out of character, given the Tom we come to know as the book progresses.) Instead, Tom adds, "It's not something you're ever likely to know for sure" (*Home*, 21). And he goes right on scolding Salty, warning him not to push things too far. It is at this point that Salty begins to suspect that Tom might be his father.

Later, when Babe insists that Salty put on some of Tom's underwear, since he has none of his own, Salty becomes adamant. Squeezing the old cotton drawers into an empty box of Epsom Salts at the back of the bathroom closet after she leaves, he defies Babe, observing that "under all that fat softness, she was a sack of cement" (*Home*, 35). That night, when Babe leaves a pair of Tom's pajamas for him, he flings them into a corner of his basement room, preferring to sleep in nothing. Salty needs to reject Tom, much as he feels that Tom rejected him.

Salty gets another view of Tom, however, when Tollybosky begins to squawk in the middle of the night. After going outside to quiet him down, Salty gets lost in the dark, unfamiliar house. Opening the wrong door, he barges into Tom and Babe's bedroom:

> Springs jounced and a lamp went on. Tom was sitting up in a ruffled pink bed beside Babe, looking like a frog on a doily. . . . "Don't you know how to knock, damn it?" Tom hissed. He seemed to be seeing for the first time, with Salty, the fluffy room full of Jesus pictures and the lamp shaped like a morning glory that flared down on his spiked hair. (*Home*, 41–42)

Both Salty and Tom are embarrassed, but the common feeling, though unwelcome at the time, is a small step toward their mutual understanding.

Salty takes another step forward when he decides that he will fix up the dilapidated Buckley Arms. Enlisting Hardy's help, he sets out to repair the roof, hopeful that more boarders will come if the place looks better, and that Tom will not need to sell it.

When Tom gets a job at the ice dock (a warehouse for the blocks of ice used in the old "ice boxes" that were the precursors of refrigerators) and brings home paint and shingles one day, the message is not lost on Salty—he realizes that Tom could have spent the money on bus tickets to rid himself of him and Mam— and he jubilantly sets to work. As he climbs up on the roof, he revels in the wind and sun, exhilarated by the height; he feels that he has a stake in the Buckley Arms. His enthusiastic foresight begins to jolt Tom out of his depressed state of mind; instead of settling into the status quo, Tom begins to see the future through Salty's eyes. At one point, he even proposes a toast to the Buckley Arms.

Shortly after this incident, Salty and Tom share an experience that tightens the bond that is slowly forming between them. Babe, worried that the job at the ice dock is too much for Tom, sends Salty to help him. The two work side by side, then share a lunch topped off by a huge watermelon. Tom even makes Salty a snow cone by pouring grape soda over ice he scrapes from the frosty coils. But when Tom accidentally locks his keys in the engine room, Salty tries to help by squeezing through a small window. As he gropes along the wall for something to hold on to, Salty's hand closes over an electrified metal box, sending shock waves through his suddenly rigid body. Engulfed in pain, he feels himself jerked out into the light.

Tom is beside himself with worry and fright, apologizing over and over as he cradles Salty in his arms. This is exactly the closeness that Salty has been yearning for, but it is over all too quickly as Tom gets back to business. Disappointed and confused, Salty wonders if in his desperate need for Tom's love he had actually intended to cause the accident.

Salty's turbulent feelings for Tom continue to rage, even when Hardy, who has guessed the truth, tries to explain to Salty why Tom cannot admit to being his father and why he is torn between his responsibilities to Salty and to Babe. Unconvinced, Salty wonders whether Tom is ashamed of him or thinks there is something wrong with him because his mother was unable to speak. No amount of soothing on Hardy's part can ease Salty's pain, as he announces venomously, "I'm never going to love him. Never. I don't care no more about him than he does me" (*Home*, 106). Of course, the reality is that they care about each other very much, but Salty's inability to understand and Tom's struggle with his conscience prevent them from developing a real father-son relationship.

Things come to a head on the Fourth of July, when Salty dresses up in Tom's old army uniform—which he and Hardy had found, and Babe had allowed him to wear—as part of a skit he and Hardy are planning. It is ironic that now Salty feels compelled to wear Tom's clothes, when earlier he recoiled from the thought of wearing Tom's underwear and pajamas. However, now that he wants to understand Tom, he thinks that wearing his clothes might help somehow, might somehow bring them closer. But Tom doesn't see it that way. Amazed when he stumbles upon Salty in his old uniform, he angrily calls him a "little scum." Salty, who has no idea what he has done wrong, is bewildered and angry. When Hardy drags him away, Salty scolds himself for expecting too much and for giving Tom a chance to love him.

When Salty runs outside and discovers Idalee watching these events through the Buckleys' window, he becomes angry and tries to shoo her off. She persists, however, and asks him why a grown man like Tom is crying. Salty chases her off, sorry she has seen Tom in such a vulnerable state. He is angry at himself for feeling sorry for Tom when he really wants to hate him. But now he sees the man "who had danced and made love to his momma" (*Home*, 150).

However, things only get worse when, after Tollybosky attacks the Eversole children, Tom and Babe give the gander away without Salty's knowledge. Determined to tell Babe Tom's secret in retaliation, Salty physically attacks Tom, who fends him off. Finally, Hardy succeeds in quelling Salty's rage by forcing him to think of the Fourth of July parade, in which Salty had hoped to win a prize. In the days that follow, though, the tension continues to increase, until news of Rose Ann's abortion finally releases something in Tom, causing his feelings to spill out—and Salty is privy to Tom's words. Sitting almost forgotten in the back seat of

Tom's car, Salty hears him tell Hardy that he has always regretted never being able to grieve properly for Dovie and has never felt free to acknowledge Salty. Later, when Salty and Tom are alone in the car, and Salty is finally beginning to understand Tom's pain, he silently accepts Tom's apology—for giving Tollybosky away, for underestimating Salty, for saying things in anger that he did not mean. On the heels of this conversation comes their search for Mam, who wanders away from the Buckley Arms; as Salty sees Tom's concern for Mam's safety, the bond between the two grows even closer. Tom's admission of love for Salty finally comes, amid the eruption of Roman candles and Fourth of July rockets, which symbolize the explosive gratitude and hope felt by Salty at Tom's long-awaited declaration.

The Search for Identity

Just as love and responsibility go hand in hand throughout the novel, so do the themes of birth and identity. Salty's birth, of course, is the catalyst for the entire story, and his search for identity is the element that advances the plot. But Salty also goes through a figurative birth—from an immature, confused boy to a more confident, understanding young man. Evidence of this new Salty appears in his conversation with the heretofore detested Idalee, as he sits with her on the roof and watches the fireworks. "Salty, you like me?" she asks. "I don't know nothing about you," he replies. "But I like you already. . . . Just because I want to," she says (*Home*, 190). When Idalee suddenly sees the light go on in her room, she flies down the ladder and across the street, fearing her father's wrath that she is not in her room. Left alone, Salty regrets not having let her light a "sparkle stick."

Parallel to Salty's figurative birth is the coming of Jo's baby son, Micah. That he is born in Salty's bed is significant, for he represents all the hopes and dreams that Salty has for himself. Moreover, Micah's presence spurs Salty on in his search for identity. At the baby's naming party, as everyone tries to help Jo to choose from the dictionary list, they discover that each name has a meaning. When Salty asks the meaning of his name, Tom replies that it means "asked for." "*Salty*?" asks Babe incredulously. "Saul," says Tom. "Saul means asked for" (*Home*, 142). Though Tom quickly dispels any suspicion about his knowing the origin of Salty's name by saying that he had gotten the information from Mam, Salty is struck by Tom's revelation. Lying in bed that night, he basks in the knowledge that he had been asked for, that his mother had wanted him. But he realizes that, in her simplicity, she would neither have looked in a book for a name nor attached any significance to a name's meaning. Someone else must have suggested the name to her, and they had decided together. "Salty. Saul T. . . . Saul Thomas" (*Home*, 144). Like Micah, Salty has a new identity, and the discovery is part of his emergence into a new life.

The birth theme also extends to the unborn, as Salty observes the conflict between Hardy and Rose Ann over their newly conceived child. Like Rose Ann, he interprets Hardy's anger at the pregnancy as evidence that he does not want the child, and Salty immediately identifies with the unborn baby, whom he calls "the bean." He wishes he could make Hardy understand how important it is to be wanted.

Though Salty is too naïve to fully understand the implications of Rose Ann's abortion, he hears Tom discussing it with Hardy, speculating on how different things would be if Dovie had done the same thing. Perhaps somewhere in himself Salty realizes that life, with all its pain and sorrow, is still better than not being born at all, that being "asked for" makes the pain bearable. "The Bean," as Salty calls him, would not have a chance to grow to maturity, but Salty would, if he could open himself to the nurturing that Tom offered.

The birth motif in *Far from Home* is evident not only through the children but through the adults as well. "I feel as new as he is," comments Jo after Micah's birth (*Home*, 123). Her decision to return with the baby to her husband in order to try again is further evidence of the "new Jo." Likewise, we sense a new Hardy McCaslin as he does some soul-searching and hops the train to go

to see Rose Ann. Tom, too, gets a second chance to love the son
he cannot publicly acknowledge, thereby fulfilling part of his own
need to be loved and gaining a new identity as a father.

Plot Structure and Imagery

In structuring the plot of *Far from Home*, Sebestyen has created
several correspondences. Babe and Tom, for example, mirror
Rose Ann and Hardy. While Babe is unable to have children and
wants them desperately, Rose Ann conceives a child and aborts
it—in part, because of failed communication, in part because the
immature Hardy refuses to take responsibility for his part in the
conception. Tom, on the other hand, wanted his child, but was
forced by circumstances to live apart from him and is tortured by
the responsibility he feels.

There is a parallel, too, between Dovie and Jo. Both bear sons
under less than ideal circumstances. Dovie is not married to Tom
and has no hope of being so, and Jo has run away from her husband because of his criminal behavior. Though Dovie is Salty's
biological mother, Jo serves as a figurative mother to him, sharing many of Dovie's most admirable qualities. Jo's decision to
return with her son to her husband parallels Dovie's dying wish
that Salty return to Tom. Jo's last words to Salty, "I don't turn
loose of people I love," might well have been spoken by Dovie, as
she wisely set in motion the father-son reunion.

In contrast to the similarities between Jo and Dovie are the dif-
ferences between Jo and Rose Ann. Both are expecting a child,
but each handles her pregnancy differently. Where Jo reaches
out to others with love and generosity, embracing the life within
her, Rose Ann draws inward, retreating to her room when she
feels threatened. She becomes pregnant not because she wants a
child but to hold her marriage together. Though we get the feeling that she and Jo are about the same age, Jo is much more
mature than Rose Ann, much more reflective and philosophical.
Though she is estranged from her husband at this crucial time in
their marriage, she never indulges in self-pity; she gives birth to

her baby alone, quietly, in the middle of the night, welcoming him lovingly. Rose Ann, on the other hand, has a devoted husband but is not strong enough or wise enough to make her marriage work. Instead, she runs away from her problems. Just as Hardy is child*like* in his love of practical jokes, she is child*ish* in her self-centeredness and inability to understand his nature.

As intriguing as Sebestyen's plot structure are the images she creates in *Far from Home*. The names she gives her characters, for example, are often sensory in nature, evoking certain feelings in the reader. "Dovie" brings to mind a soft, lovely, white bird—the symbol of peace. "Salty," on the other hand, conjures an image of tangy coarseness—perhaps of a quick tongue and a stubborn nature. "Babe," as mentioned earlier, is a name deliberately designed to evoke images of fat softness and childlike dependency. "Hardy" brings to mind the sound of laughter—a "hearty" laugh—as well as a certain sturdiness, an ability to endure. Descriptions like "Jo Miller came bumping slowly downstairs like a lost balloon" (*Home*, 68) are examples of Sebestyen's effective use of figurative language.

Significant, too, is the 1920s "feel" of the novel. Tom Buckley mentions several times that he's not doing well financially, and Rose Ann has a recurring dream about hard times ahead. "There's no food," she says. "Or sunlight. It's gray, cold gray, and I hear children making little thin cries" (*Home*, 88). As James Holmstrand points out in his review of *Far from Home*, "America, without acknowledging it, is on the brink of depression."[4] Sebestyen creates a strong sense of place and time in *Far from Home*, frequently sprinkling cultural idioms throughout the novel. Tom tells Salty to "cut out the razzmatazz" (*Home*, 19), Babe calls Hardy a "bamboozler" (*Home*, 31), and Hardy describes Rose Ann's dream as "the bee's knees"(*Home*, 73). Reference to Hoot Gibson movies, the Katzenjammer Kids, and songs like "Yes, We Have No Bananas" abound, as do discussions of fads like flagpole sitting and yo-yo marathons. Evidence of Sebestyen's careful research, these details lend authentic flavor to the story, expanding the setting in a way that enriches the novel.

Critical Reception

Though *Far from Home* did not receive quite the critical acclaim
of *Words by Heart*, reviews were overwhelmingly positive. Patricia
Lee Gauch, writing in the *New York Times Book Review*, stated
that "Ouida Sebestyen lets her character [Salty] touch the others
honestly 'with a little bluster of hope' and produces an aching
irony, for it is July 1929, the end of an era."[5] *Kirkus Reviews*
noted that "Sebestyen gives her touching characters dimension
and fills the Buckley Arms with convincing life and a special
atmosphere as the motley cast coheres to form a household."[6]
Booklist called the novel "uneven but affecting,"[7] while the
Bulletin of the Center for Children's Books bestowed the ultimate
compliment by comparing it favorably to an American classic:

> This is not a childlike story, but should have some of the same
> kind of appeal that *To Kill a Mockingbird* has had to many ado-
> lescent and pre-adolescent readers: a vividly created microcosm
> of society, an abundance of sentiment without sentimentality,
> and a protagonist who is drawn with compassionate percipi-
> ence.[8]

At the end of *Far from Home* we see Salty writing his name in
light with his Fourth of July sparkler. It has not occurred to him
that he might well be "the child from this house [who] will
change the world," but the implication is there, as is the hope for
the future that Salty feels. Grim times are ahead, but this is a
new Salty.

5. *IOU's*

A confused son on the brink of young adulthood. A mother disinherited by her father and deserted by her husband. A dingy little rented house. A rather bleak picture, really, and one that conjures up images of unhappiness and discontent.

Yet this is not at all the case for Annie and Stowe Garrett who, despite their modest means, maintain an affectionate, cheerful mother-son relationship firmly grounded in love and hope. When we first meet them, Stowe and Annie are on their way out the door, running late, headed for the grocery store, when a phone call from Annie's cousin in Oklahoma changes Stowe's life. Clutching the receiver, aware that Annie is waiting for him in the car, Stowe learns that his dying grandfather, from whom his mother is estranged, has asked to see him. Perplexed that the old man asked for him but not for Annie, his own daughter, Stowe becomes indignant, vowing not to go to Oklahoma unless Annie is welcome, too.

This incident sets in motion a plot that forces thirteen-year-old Stowe to confront many obstacles in his struggle for independence and self-realization. His close relationship with his mother is both a blessing and a curse. Determined to protect her from further hurt, he feels compelled to be there for her emotionally and to help her eke out their meager living. In addition to mowing lawns and delivering papers, he helps her babysit young children in their home and even goes along to assist with caring for a group of children in a church nursery—all the while embarrassed by the taunts of his friend Brownie, who can't understand why

Stowe spends so much time with Annie. But Stowe enjoys her company and feels secure in the special relationship they share. They communicate well, and they like many of the same things— long trips in Horseless, their beat-up pickup, mountains, picnics, even underground tunnels ripe for exploring.

Sebestyen creates a mother-son relationship that lends credibility to Stowe's ambivalent feelings. He loves his mother and is fiercely loyal to her, yet he feels the pull of other interests, other desires. In some ways he wants to be like Brownie, impulsive and daring, unconcerned about what his parents think. And he's increasingly aware that Karla, the girl across the street who was his first real friend, is now more interested in makeup and hairstyles, leaving him behind in his boyhood. Hoping for some magical deliverance from a life that he finds increasingly distressing, Stowe enters sweepstakes contests, convinced that one day he will be a winner and will build his and Annie's dream house. In his confusion and frustration he sometimes lashes out at Annie, blaming her for their plight, asking her why she does not get a real job and why she does not marry again.

It is during one of these heated discussions that Stowe blurts out the truth about the phone call, engendering in Annie a reaction first of shock, then of resolve. She must return to Oklahoma to see her father again, to make amends. But Stowe resists, nursing the hurt and resentment he feels toward the man who has shut them out of his life for thirteen years.

However, after Stowe nearly loses Brownie as a friend when he accuses him of thievery, Stowe has a change of heart and realizes that people need a chance to show they care. When he arrives in Oklahoma with Annie and learns that his grandfather has passed away that morning, Stowe thinks long and hard about love, death, and the future. He thinks about his own father, and he vows not to repeat the family history. When Annie decides not to honor her family's wish that she and Stowe settle in Oklahoma, Stowe is jubilant, looking forward now to their life in the shadow of the mountains they love, confident that he can handle the future.

Autobiography and Character

Sebestyen admits that *IOU's* is probably her most autobiographical work. The mother-son relationship is a theme that permeates the novel, reflecting in many ways the relationship between Sebestyen and her own son Corbin. "A lot of the things that happened to the mother and son were things we've gone through," she says, though she quickly points out that the alienation between Annie and her father is purely fiction.

Annie's voice many times echoes Sebestyen's, and the two have several things in common. Both are single parents who value human relationships over material things. Annie has been content with their hand-to-mouth existence because it has enabled her to be with Stowe as he was growing up. Like Sebestyen, she depends on babysitting jobs and crafts to provide an income, taking in extra children and working longer hours when the two of them need more money. Just as Sebestyen and Corbin made do for many years with an old station wagon well past its prime, Annie and Stowe consider their pickup truck Horseless indispensable. Perhaps the most striking similarities between author and character are their shared love of nature and their desire to create. At one point in the novel, Annie and Stowe discuss their "dream place," a piece of land with trees and a house they will build themselves. Mother and son share the dream in fiction and in life. At this writing, Sebestyen has recently moved from Colorado to Texas's hill country, with the help of her son, in order to be closer to nature—and hopefully to write more novels.

Another aspect of the parent-child relationship, more universal than idiosyncratic, takes a slight twist in *IOU's*. Parents are usually protective of their children, and Annie exhibits this quality to a certain extent. But it is really Stowe who has the strong protective instinct in this relationship. At the very beginning of the novel, as noted earlier, he tries to shield Annie from the knowledge that her ailing father has asked for his presence, but not hers. Feeling guilty at not telling her about the phone call, he thinks:

Maybe he owed her the news that her dad was better. Feeling well enough to have Cousin Harold for a visitor just a few hours ago. But how could he tell her that part without telling the rest and adding more pain to the pain she already felt?[1]

Stowe worries about his mother and feels responsible for her happiness. One evening, after helping Annie babysit a group of children in a church nursery, he finds himself in the main part of the church, wishing he could pray, wanting to tell someone that he feels a debt to his mother, that he cannot let her down. He feels a serious responsibility to make up for his father's and grandfather's neglect.

Indeed, the title of the novel reflects Stowe's feelings. First conceived as *I Owe You*, it was later changed by Sebestyen and her editor Melanie Kroupa to *IOU's*. Kroupa explains why in a memo:

> IOU is a symbol that kids know and understand—it is a kind of shorthand that suggests a tension of a sort. It fits the book more appropriately in the plural, for the story is one of many IOU's between various characters.[2]

Stowe's protective feelings toward his mother are really a source of conflict for him as he experiences the normal insecurities and frustrations of adolescence. For example, early in the novel he becomes extremely upset when Annie is caught short of money at the grocery store. As they wait in the checkout line, and Annie asks him if he has any change, his face burns with embarrassment as he feels the stares of other shoppers. Rushing out to the car, he is angry at his mother for putting them in such an awkward position.

Stowe feels uncomfortable, too, about the teasing he gets from Brownie, a boy whose own parents leave him to fend for himself. When Brownie taunts Stowe about babysitting little kids, Stowe insists he does it because he *wants* to, not because he *has* to. When Annie invites herself along to explore a mine tunnel with the two boys, Stowe worries that Brownie will think she is spoiling their fun. And when Brownie comes up with the idea to "tar and feather" Karla, Stowe balks: "Mothers don't go for stuff like that" he says. "Which mothers?" Brownie asks. "Karla's mom thinks it's a hot idea." "Ours might not, though," answers Stowe. "Mine won't know about it," Brownie replies, implying that, once again, Stowe must get permission from his mother for every little thing (*IOU's*, 109). Stowe's decision finally to go along with the prank—even to provide the shaving cream they would use as "tar"—is an attempt at independence, a message to Brownie as well as to Annie, that he is his own person.

This desire to break free of parental influence is closely connected to the coming-of-age theme that comes through strongly in *IOU's*. Throughout the novel, Stowe struggles with the knowledge that he is changing, a realization that he simultaneously embraces and resists. This conflict is especially apparent in his relationship with Karla, his longtime friend. Watching her whiz past on the back of a stranger's motorcycle, blonde hair flying, Stowe is resentful and critical. "Her dad let her get her ears pierced," he tells Brownie. When Brownie replies, "Oh, pathetic, . . . two more holes in her head," Stowe adds, "And even more junk on her face than before. Eyelashes like on a camel. She looks like she's dipped in batter, ready to cook" (*IOU's*, 34). But later, when the three of them take a wild go-cart ride that ends in a crash, Stowe rushes to Karla's aid, self-conscious in his attempts to dust her off, his hands noticing the new "slopes" of her body. Later, folding newspapers, he covertly watches her sunbathe, "glancing over each time the pink bikini rotates in the sun" (*IOU's*, 57). He wonders whether he, too, has changed, and he worries that, if he has not, he will be "stalled like an old car while everyone else his age [is] burning rubber getting past the awkwardness and ignorance and on with living" (*IOU's*, 58). When he goes over and tries to make conversation with Karla, she shoos him off for blocking the sun, and a sadness, as though he has lost something, overtakes him.

However, even when he and Brownie attack Karla with ketchup and feathers for reneging on her promise to bake cookies for their picnic, Stowe takes little pleasure in the prank and feels a sadness at the change in their relationship. When Annie points out that people mature at different rates, and that Karla is moving into "new country" faster than he is, Stowe speculates that what may really have angered him was that Karla bravely took off for that unknown territory without him.

Another incident in Stowe's emotional growth occurs when he and Annie travel to Oklahoma. As they ride together in the old pickup, they talk about Stowe's father. Annie admits that she is grateful to the man for rescuing her from Maydell, Oklahoma, and for giving her Stowe as a legacy. Later, after learning of his grandfather's death, Stowe feels guilty for keeping Annie away, and he begins to think seriously about love and death, and about his own father. In a burst of emotion, he apologizes to Annie for not telling her about the phone call, sorry that he did not give her the chance to make amends with her father before he died.

Stowe's realization that his grandfather really did love Annie in his own way and his resulting decision to make contact with his own father are significant steps on the road to that "new country" which he both fears and anticipates. His literal journey from the familiar Colorado mountains to the strange Oklahoma landscape and back symbolizes the figurative journey from childhood to young adulthood that he is just beginning.

Character Development and Relationships

One of Sebestyen's real talents as a writer is her ability to create strong, believable characters, people whom readers recognize and grow to care about. As Dick Abrahamson and Betty Carter point out, "the strength of *IOU's* is in the character development and the relationships among characters."[3] More specifically, Arielle North, writing in the *St. Louis Post Dispatch*, comments:

> The characters in *IOU's* reflect Sebestyen's incredible perceptivity. She knows how ambivalent, changeable and complex humans can be, and what havoc divided loyalties can create. She is aware of the frequent contradictions between surface appearances and inner thoughts, of the tenuous balance in even the most openhearted relationships and of the thin line between supportive love and overdependence.[4]

Stowe Garrett is a perfect example of the kind of ambivalent, changeable character that North talks about. Caught on the cusp between childhood and adulthood, he struggles with the dilemma of wanting to break free of Annie's influence and yet feeling secure in her love. Stowe, though usually kind and considerate, also has a vindictive side, which is revealed in his solitary decision to hold out against his grandfather, as the old man had held out against him and Annie. Thoughtful and cautious by nature, Stowe yearns to be impulsive like Brownie, to act first and think later rather than second-guessing Annie's reaction to everything he does. At the same time, though, his bond with Annie is cemented in a way of which he may not even be aware: both he and his mother were deserted by their fathers, and they take refuge in each other—a need that Stowe will have to overcome if he is ever to break free.

In addition to the conflicts inherent in his relationship with his mother, Sebestyen effectively uses another plot device to develop Stowe's character. An incident involving a one-hundred-dollar bill helps to reveal aspects of Stowe's personality that are not readily apparent in his relationship with his mother. Unlike Annie, he considers money important, believing that it can solve all their problems. Sebestyen illustrates this and Stowe's naiveté through his conviction that he will one day "hit it big" in one of the many contests he enters. When he finds a twenty-dollar bill and adds it to the other money he has secretly saved, he has a total of one hundred dollars, an astronomical sum to him. Going to the bank to exchange the money for a one-hundred-dollar bill is an important event for Stowe, for it makes his decision to display the bill on his bedroom wall with some bogus money seem all the more foolish, given the fact that Annie's young charges frequently nap in his bedroom. When the one-hundred-dollar bill disappears, Stowe's lack of good judgement reveals him as a normal thirteen-year-old who perhaps worries too much about being an anomaly.

Stowe's relationship with Brownie also helps to reveal him as a normal adolescent. At one point he decides to carry out Annie's instructions with a vengeance by unblocking all at once the dam he and Brownie have built, causing a deluge. As he and Brownie are carried along by the surging water, scraping against rocks and lumber, Stowe thinks to Annie, "Okay, this is what you wanted" (*IOU's*, 48). His spiteful action is childish—and dangerous—but it is his way of rebelling against his mother and showing Brownie that he is in charge.

Once again, revenge is the order of the day in another revealing incident, one that occurs when Stowe and Brownie carry out their plan to "tar and feather" Karla. The scene is reminiscent of two little boys chasing a little girl down the street. Shouting and screaming, squirting ketchup and throwing feathers, at first Stowe is caught up in the action. "We declared war on you, Karla," he says, handing Brownie a water-filled balloon from their arsenal (*IOU's*, 110). But somehow Stowe senses that things are not quite right.

> He cackled. He was doing something crazy again, just like Brownie. With reckless elation he clamped one arm around Karla's waist and felt the breath whoosh out of her. For a second he was aware that, one handed, he could hurt her if he wanted to. The sadness filled him, for something ending. He liked her so much, and they couldn't play that way much longer. (*IOU's*, 111)

Stowe's ambivalent feelings about growing up are certainly believable in a thirteen-year-old, but there is perhaps one flaw in his characterization. In the midst of his regret at keeping Annie away from her dying father, his epiphany about his own father seems almost to stretch credibility for one so young and confused about his own identity. Sebestyen describes how Stowe suddenly realizes that he has just crossed a point in his life where he understood that his selfish actions could result in his father's becoming like his grandfather. This sudden insight on the part of a thirteen-year-old suggests a maturity that Stowe does not yet possess in the novel. To imply that the change happens quickly is perhaps gratuitous and a little disappointing to the reader who, up to now, has believed in the validity of Stowe's character. This sudden leap toward maturity does serve a purpose, though, for it justifies Annie's decision to let Stowe drive the pickup alone down the deserted road as she walks on ahead. This incident, which is symbolic of Stowe's growing independence, reaffirms Annie's trust and confidence in her son, and it reveals Stowe's willingness to face the future.

Annie, too, looks forward to what life will bring. She tells Stowe, "There's a marvelous made-up word in a book called *Finnigan's Wake*. Gracehopers. . . . We're gracehopers" (*IOU's*, 186). Though Stowe does not really understand this, the passage, and the word, tell a great deal about Annie's character—loving, gracious, hopeful, possessed of a moral strength that she passes on to her son. In a review of the book, Colby Rodowsky states:

> It is a credit to Sebestyen's skill as a writer that through Stowe we are able to see Annie as a person who is eminently human: lonely, loving, at times scared, tough, afraid to feel too deeply.[5]

But some readers have criticized Annie as "too good to be true," too consistently understanding and wise. In a letter to Sebestyen discussing revision of the manuscript, Melanie Kroupa writes:

> The main element that has been brought to my attention by several new readers is the characterization of Annie. She is a strong, interesting character to be sure, but . . . she comes across [as] being so consistently understanding, so constantly ready to offer prescriptions for rectitude that, along with her unfailing goodness and ability to see the other side, [her coming across this way] becomes annoying to the reader and begins to seem unrealistic. She *must* get tired and cranky sometimes![6]

By way of explanation, Sebestyen replies:

> [W]hat we've got here is a sincerely bumbly-type possessive mother who's trying not to be, and a loving son who's trying to let her have him as long as she needs him, at the same time that he's taking his first steps into independence.[7]

Even after Sebestyen made some revisions, though, some readers remain unconvinced. A review of *IOU's* in *Kirkus Reviews* states that it is "hard not to find Annie and Stowe a little cloying and idealized in a slightly sickly way."[8]

If Annie is too good in the novel, though, it is a minor flaw, one that perhaps even works in her favor. While it would be easy for a woman who has been repeatedly hurt and rejected to harbor anger and bitterness, Annie's refusal to do so strengthens her character and provides her son with a positive image of "woman" that he will carry with him into his adult life. Of course, there must be times when she becomes upset or sad, but having Stowe witness her anger and her tears would serve only to increase his guilt and sense of responsibility toward her—which would not necessarily advance the plot in any way.

Perhaps the focus on Annie's "goodness" has been misplaced. Perhaps, instead, more attention should be paid to her strength of character and her success in raising her child. For thirteen years she has gone it alone, and she has performed quite admirably. Though she and Stowe have only very basic comforts, she makes sure that they are rich in love, companionship, and care. Not one to lament what they lack in material luxuries, she teaches Stowe by example that happiness lies in more important things like friends, family, and the beauty of nature. And Stowe is an apt pupil: at one point, Annie asks Stowe what he plans to do while he is waiting to "hit it big" in one of his contests. "Thrift store clothes and cringing and skimping, just to see a mountain out your window?" she asks. "Sure," he replies. "Even rich people can't buy mountains for their windows" (*IOU's*, 18).

Annie is a proud woman. Though she accepts the mysterious monthly check from her father, she refuses to ask her estranged husband for financial support. When Stowe questions her about this, she replies, "I guess the difference is that [my father] doesn't owe it to us" (*IOU's*, 19). Annie's mixture of strength, love, and pride merits more attention than her much-criticized goodness in the novel; readers who look closely will see that Annie has her faults, too—as she is the first to admit.

Minor Characters

An exploration of *IOU's* would not be complete without some discussion of the minor characters in the novel, notably Brownie and Karla. Though these two young people are fictional, they are based on friends of Sebestyen's son, Corbin, and she uses them in interesting ways—as catalysts for Stowe's emotional growth in the novel.

Brownie is, of course, a foil to Stowe: impulsive where Stowe is cautious, daring where Stowe is fearful, superficial where Stowe is introspective, lacking in parental love where Stowe sometimes has more than he wants. Stowe is aware of these contrasts, and, as he searches for his own identity, he frequently measures himself against Brownie. When he does so, the reader can see in whose favor the scale tips—though it is not always apparent that Stowe comes to this realization. In spite of the contrasts, though, Stowe and Brownie have one thing in common: both are honest. When Stowe accuses Brownie of stealing his one-hundred-dollar bill, a serious rift opens in their friendship, leading to some soul-searching on Stowe's part. When he learns the truth, that one of Annie's young charges cut the money in pieces to share and that Annie flushed it down the toilet, thinking it was fake, he humbles himself and apologizes to Brownie, thereby taking another step toward maturity. (Sebestyen reveals that the one-hundred-dollar bill incident really did happen, though the mystery of its disappearance was never solved. She felt that she had to create a solution in the novel, so as not to leave her readers wondering.)

Just as Brownie serves an important purpose in the novel, so does Karla, Stowe's potential love interest. Time and again, Sebestyen portrays Karla as a pubescent young woman who is leaving her prepubescent male friends behind. Her interest in riding on a motorcycle, wearing makeup, polishing her nails, and generally attending to matters of growing up highlights Stowe's reluctance to move into that "new country," as Sebestyen calls it. His fondness for Karla, his longtime friend, confuses him as he begins to notice her physical and emotional changes. Sebestyen portrays Stowe's confusion effectively, communicating the love-hate feelings that Stowe experiences. His and Brownie's decision to "tar and feather" Karla is a perfect example of this: amid the glee, Stowe feels a sadness that he does not fully understand. Though Sebestyen drew on another real-life incident in creating this scene, she takes it far beyond simple shenanigans and uses it instead to develop Stowe's character further.

Ultimately, it is Stowe's friendship with Brownie and Karla that helps him to understand and accept the situation with his dying grandfather. When he and Brownie apologize to Karla for the ketchup and feather massacre, she accepts their apology, and Stowe basks in their renewed friendship, thinking to himself, "I love you. . . . I love us for being back together again" (*IOU's*, 146). As he realizes the importance of forgiveness, he thinks of his grandfather's overture in asking to see him, and as a result he realizes that he must give the old man the same chance that Karla gave to him and Brownie. Unfortunately, his decision comes too late for his grandfather; nevertheless, Stowe benefits from his newfound knowledge. As a review in the *Horn Book Magazine* points out, "The resolution is neither glib nor simple but rather reflective of reality where large losses are sometimes followed by small advances."[9]

In *IOU's* Sebestyen has created yet another novel that celebrates strong family relationships and champions the value of friendship. Her dedication of the book to her son Corbin and his friends, then, seems most appropriate:

> To the S and S Company and all the others
> who shared their thirteenth summer

6. *On Fire*

Authors are sometimes leery of writing sequels to successful novels. How can the second book measure up to the first? Will readers be disappointed? Are some characters and events better left alone? Some novelists feel that reader demand dictates the writing of a sequel. But in the case of Ouida Sebestyen, it was her own desire to tell the other side of the story, the dark side, that prompted her to write *On Fire*, a companion novel rather than a sequel to *Words by Heart*. "I wanted readers to understand the Haneys," she says. "They had their story, too."

The central character in *On Fire* is twelve-year-old Sammy Haney, whose older brother Tater (Henry Tate, Jr.) shot and killed the saintly Ben Sills in the earlier novel, *Words by Heart*. Unaware of his brother's crime, and badly in need of a male role model, Sammy idolizes Tater and strives to follow in his footsteps. When their drunken father, Pap, is jailed, Tater decides to take a job working in a Colorado coal mine to support his sickly mother and her other children. When Sammy tries to go along, Tater orders him to stay with the family to help take their father's place.

Enter Yankee Belew, an orphaned miner's daughter who has come to town to bury properly her older sister, a prostitute, and who, by chance, meets Sammy and Tater in the sheriff's office. Later, after befriending Sammy and learning of his brother's plans, she warns him of the danger in working in the mines. Tater unknowingly has been hired as a strikebreaker, and Yankee, whose brother was killed for his union activity, has seen the violence firsthand. Having come into a modest sum of money left by her sister, Yankee pays for Sammy's train ticket so that he may follow Tater to Pegler, Colorado, where Yankee lives. It is here that the story gains momentum, as Sammy tries to find Tater and convince him of the danger.

Woven throughout the drama of the search and of Sammy's increasing emotional ties to Yankee and her baby nephew, Charlie, is Tater's barely disguised turmoil over his father's failures and his own vile act of murder, committed four months earlier. As Sammy begins to see the reality of Tater's deed, he at first refuses to believe that his brother could do such a thing, then rationalizes that it was only a black man that Tater killed. Gradually, however, he comes to see the darkness of Tater's soul—something he wants no part of—and he feels the bond between them break.

As Tater continues his trail of dirty deeds, setting fire to the boardinghouse and hiring on to kill Galen Stoker, the mine owner, Sammy feels compelled to warn Stoker, who was once in love with Yankee's now-dead sister. Thinking that Sammy is out for money, Stoker at first rejects his warning but gradually softens when Sammy tells him about Yankee and Charlie. Resigned to the danger he lives with daily, Stoker helps Sammy to see the folly of revenge and retaliation, even though the man knows it will continue. When Tater decides to give himself up rather than shoot Stoker, and even asks Stoker for a job, the mine owner agrees to consider it. Back in Yankee's room, where Sammy has brought him for warmth, Tater is remorseful, saying that he wanted Ben Sills to be right about him when Sills saved his life— he wanted his life to be worth saving. Ever kindhearted, Yankee comforts a sobbing Tater as Sammy looks hopefully toward the future, making a conscious decision to leave the past behind.

Though *On Fire* still illuminates the racism that existed in *Words by Heart*, it is primarily a novel of class struggle. Tater, though he is considered "poor white trash" by some, still feels himself superior to the immigrants who flock to work in the mines. He frequently refers to them as "dagos," "wops," and "bohunks," dehumanizing them in a way that reflects his own upbringing. Though his mother was probably once a woman of some gentility (she treasures a teapot that was a family heirloom from Londonderry), it is apparent that his father, a crude bigot, was the dominant force in the family. Indeed, his mother, Mrs. Tate, does not even merit a first name: her two sons refer to her only as "she."

Setting

Telling the story through Sammy's eyes was Sebestyen's way of dealing with her limited knowledge of mining. Years before, she had explored a silver mine, and she did a great deal of reading about mines before she wrote *On Fire*, but she felt she was certainly no expert. Using Sammy's point of view as a storytelling device enabled her to work within the boundaries of her own knowledge while having Sammy imagine what it would be like to work underground.

The ways in which Tater and the other workers hired as strikebreakers are manipulated is indicative of the exploitation that existed at the time. Sebestyen based the novel on a real event, the Ludlow Massacre, which took place in the coal camps of southeastern Colorado on April 20, 1914. Outraged at the poor working conditions, mine workers went on strike in protest, presenting the owners with a list of demands, none of which were met. Violence broke out, and the militia was called in. Strikers were characterized as "ignorant, lawless, savage South-European peasants; unassimilable aliens to whom liberty means license."[1] The militia set afire the tent colony erected by the strikers and looted the tents as the camp went up in flames.

Unions had little power in those days, as Sebestyen illustrates in *On Fire* when Yankee's brother Mick, a union activist, is murdered while giving a speech. The conflict between union and management takes on a sinister hue, as men armed with clubs and guns confront each other openly and murders are plotted behind closed doors. Through it all, the socioeconomic status of people like Galen Stoker contrasts sharply with that of people like Tater, Sammy, and Yankee. The "haves" successfully suppress the "have-nots," and the oppressed continue to hate the oppressors. Tater, who watches Stoker's family thrive while his own mother, brothers, and sisters are homeless and starving, embodies this hatred.

Setting is especially important in this novel. The year is 1911. As Marjorie Lewis points out in her review of the book, it was "a time when there were no economic safety nets, when children worked side by side with adults, when labor was locked in combat with management."[2] As a piece of historical fiction, *On Fire* accurately depicts a time when life was cheap and children were robbed of their childhood. Events take place in February, the dead of winter, reinforcing the sense of hopelessness that pervades the story. The frozen landscape yields only mud, which threatens literally to suck the Haneys and Yankee into its mire, just as they are figuratively pulled down by their unfortunate circumstances. Warmth is hard to come by. The Haneys, who have no home, camp around a fire. Even Yankee's small room has little heat, since she cannot afford the coal needed for the stove. Outside the boardinghouse, the miners must slog through the frozen slush to use the privy.

In a more diffuse sense, Sebestyen uses subtler aspects of setting to good effect. Even though some of the novel's events take place in daylight, there is an overpowering sense of darkness in the book. The story opens in the middle of the night, as Sammy and Tater hear their father stealing away from their camp as he heads for town. They follow him in the darkness, stealing meat from a delivery wagon parked in the dark alley behind a boardinghouse. The train ride to Pegler is made at night, with Sammy staring through the train's grimy windows. Yankee's living quarters are bleak—"a cold narrow room above the barbershop" with "dingy walls and empty bookcases."[3] Sammy's attempt to save Stoker from Tater's bullet takes place at night, with "snow . . . falling in a white gloom where the hills should have been" (*On Fire*, 187). Even the final scene, hopeful as it is, occurs in the dark loft above Yankee's room, where Mrs. Haney and her children are asleep.

As counterpoint to these dark images, Sebestyen periodically interjects images of heat and flame in the novel, illuminating certain events as a means of underscoring their importance in the story. Early in the book Sammy and Tater visit their father in jail, where Pap calls Tater "pig slop" and yells after him, "They'll burn you, boy" (*On Fire*, 20). Shortly after, as they watch the sheriff lock up the jail, Tater points out to Sammy that Pap is alone now in the building, and he wonders what would happen if the place went up in flames. This incident foreshadows what will later occur in Pegler, introducing the element of fire in its most literal and dangerous sense.

Sammy worries about fire, too, especially the fires of hell. When the preacher presiding over the burial of Yankee's sister warns of "the bottomless pit of perdition," Sammy envisions a hell even more terrible than the one his father has told him about. "The preacher had made him see it, gaping, and all at once he was afraid for Tater" (*On Fire*, 41). Sammy is concerned about Tater's reckless behavior. Going down into the depths of the mine seems to him like a descent into hell.

The image of flame surfaces again on the train ride to Pegler, when Yankee and Sammy look out the window and see the glow of fire where the land and sky join. Sammy becomes anxious as the train seems to approach the blaze. Watching the smoke rise as if from an inferno, he wonders if those flames might have originated in hell. As the train moves on and passengers settle into sleep, Sammy feels compelled to tell Yankee, "My brother killed somebody" (*On Fire*, 68).

Tater's earlier speculation about what might happen if the jail housing his father were to catch fire is brought to mind again when Sammy is shaken awake early one morning by the fire bell. As the rumble of explosions rattles the windows, his worst fears are realized. "Oh, Jesus," he says softly. "A building blowed up" (*On Fire*, 123). Hoping it isn't the boardinghouse, Sammy runs through the streets and rounds a corner, only to see the huge building ablaze. Screaming "My brother's in there!" he tries to get through the crowd, to no avail. His only hope is that the men had already left for the mine before the fire broke out. Suddenly aware that he has run through the snow wearing no shoes, Sammy follows Yankee's advice to go back home and finish dressing; but as he climbs the stairs to their room, he encounters Tater hiding in the darkness and is appalled to learn that his brother is responsible for starting the fire. Though Sammy is at first incredulous at Tater's revelation, he neverthless admires Tater's boldness and his decision to switch to the union side. Gradually, though, he realizes that if Tater had set the fire fifteen minutes later, Yankee and Charlie would have been in the boardinghouse, where Yankee had recently taken a job in the kitchen. This further confuses him, as he feels torn between defending Tater and protecting Yankee. Later, Sammy and Yankee watch the boardinghouse as it continues to burn:

> The roof had fallen. The blaze still ate slowly, like an animal gnawing the bones of something it had killed. . . . little brooding knots of watchers still gazed into the fire's smoldering depths. "All they had," Yankee said unexpectedly. "All they'd brought from their homeland." . . . Perplexed, he stared into the dreamily rising smoke. Were they sad? How could they be? They were foreign, most of them—they couldn't even talk American. (*On Fire*, 134–35)

Later still, as they lie in the dark, waiting for sleep, Tater tells Sammy that he felt "alive" while setting the fire, a juxtaposition of life and death imagery that Sebestyen uses to call attention to the horror of Tater's act. Sammy feels "the icicle-and-heat strangeness" of Tater's words, all the while wondering if he would share in Tater's gloating had Yankee not been nearby in the dark room, possibly listening.

Sammy, Tater, and Yankee

Sammy, the novel's protagonist, grows in several ways. At first he is blindly devoted to Tater, so needful of someone to look up to that he is unable to see his brother's faults. He feels so much a part of Tater that he cannot begin to conceive of their separation.

When Tater decides to follow Pap into town, Sammy scrambles after him. When Tater filches meat from the delivery wagon, Sammy is right behind him, feeling "a singing jolt of joy" as he and Tater break into a run after their theft. When Tater signs up to work in the mines, Sammy wants to sign up, too, even though Tater orders him to stay with their family, even threatening to beat him if he disobeys. Sammy's stubborn allegiance to his brother is what prompts him to hop the train to Pegler so he can warn Tater of the impending danger. Young and naïve, he doesn't think of the danger in which he is placing himself by going to a strange town alone. When Sammy finally locates Tater at the boardinghouse, and Tater acknowledges him, he feels content: "They were together. . . . His world had order again. He knew what to do" (*On Fire*, 100–107).

As the story progresses, however, Sammy becomes more and more influenced by Yankee, whose honesty and kindness make her quite the opposite of Tater. He sees her selflessness as she accepts full responsibility for her sister's child. He experiences her generosity when she buys him a train ticket with the little money she has, then takes him in so that he will have a place to sleep. He even finds himself "unbuttoning his private thoughts" to Yankee, letting her know of his fears for Tater. Sammy's ambivalence is apparent, as he first tries to justify Tater's murdering Ben Sills, then questions the justice of it, finally rationalizing that Tater was only trying to help his father keep his job.

As Sammy becomes increasingly torn between his loyalty to Tater and what his conscience tells him about right and wrong, his confusion grows. At one point in the story, he resists the urge to steal from an old man because Yankee believes in him and he does not want to betray her trust. Later, when he learns that Tater set the boardinghouse fire, he finally comes to terms with his relationship with Tater. When Tater indicates that he will continue this kind of criminal activity, "Sammy [feels] the bond between them break and dump him slowly into emptiness" (*On Fire*, 158). He resists Tater's effort to pull him close as they lie next to each other, waiting for sleep.

Listening to Yankee, Sammy begins to realize how much she loved her brother Mick, giving a name to that look he sees on her face when she talks about him. Later in the story he sees that look again, when Yankee cradles the sobbing Tater.

Though Sammy's growth through the story is believable, Tater's sudden change of heart at the end of the novel may not be quite as convincing. A review in the *Bulletin of the Center for Children's Books* charges that "Tater is vicious, bigoted, and selfish, and his conversion to ethical propriety comes as the one unconvincing aspect of a story in which his venality, although unpleasant, has been a consistent note."[4]

A closer look at the novel, however, does reveal glimpses of a Tater that Sebestyen wants us to see—an angry, vulnerable sixteen-year-old whose false bravado is a defense against a society that he feels is unfair. When their father sneaks away in the middle of the night and Sammy wants to go after him, Tater remarks, "I'm tired of looking after him like I was his father. For once I just wanted to lay there and not care what the hell he done" (*On Fire*, 6). Seeing some trainmen eating breakfast through the hotel dining room windows, Tater says, "I'll do that someday . . . and hold out a twenty-dollar bill between two fingers, like I didn't care if it fell to the floor or what" (*On Fire*, 6).

When Tater encounters his drunken father in jail, the exchange between the two reveals disgust and hatred, as Pap reaches through the bars and yanks Tater so hard that his nose smashes against the steel bars and begins to bleed. "Don't you lip me, boy . . . and don't you blame me for what you brought on yourself and the whole bunch of us with your craziness," he yells. "Name of God, Pap," Tater whispers. "I done it for you. . . . so you could stay. So you could work. Damned if you're going to call it craziness, what I done." "Be damned, then," hisses Pap (*On Fire*, 17–18). At this point, Tater knows he's on his own to struggle with the memory of Ben Sills's murder. His self-loathing is apparent when the sheriff tells them that if they do not get out of town, they will wish they had never been born. "Hell, I wish that already," Tater replies (*On Fire*, 23).

Tater frequently has nightmares about the murder, which Sammy overhears. Haunted by the fact that Sills tried to help him, even though the man was mortally wounded, Tater laments that he did not make "a good clean shot." When Sammy asks him why he did it, Tater contradicts what he told his father. "I thought it might make me different. Like maybe bigger," he says. "But it didn't, I guess. . . . Now sometimes I wish the law would just take me. Just fry me and get it over with. But I guess that's too easy, too. You don't get to just die" (*On Fire*, 156–57). Mulling over in his mind the fact that Lena Sills and her father saved his life, Tater is tormented by the guilt he tries to bury.

Another clue to Tater's character that might help legitimize his redemption is his genuine concern for his mother and younger siblings. A tender moment occurs just before he leaves for the mines, when his mother traces the scar on his forehead and, softly crying, gives him her blessing. Visibly touched, Tater remains resolute. Later in the novel, after Mrs. Haney and the children come to Pegler, Tater's anger at Pap flares again, as he feels protective of his family, especially his mother, who he feels has been "used" by his father. He resents Pap's saddling him with this responsibility, yet he still seeks work to help his family survive. He does not abandon them, as his father had.

Typical of a young man deprived of his childhood, Tater has other desires that have not been fulfilled. At sixteen, he certainly notices girls and thinks about sex. His vulgar comments upon learning that Yankee's sister was a prostitute illustrate this. After the burial he tries to hitch a ride to town on the gravediggers' wagon. "Laid her for good?" he asks the men, who chuckle at his innuendo (*On Fire*, 53). Though his meaning escapes Sammy, it is not lost on the reader. Frequently Tater makes snide references to Sammy's "getting lucky" even while he is too young to take sexual advantage of his relationship with Yankee.

Tater's own reaction to Yankee is confused, as he seems drawn to her yet insults her at every turn. Calling her "Miss Doodle," he mocks her honesty and laughs at her refusal to eat food he has stolen for them. Lying in the dark falling asleep, knowing that Yankee is within earshot, Tater chuckles, "Bet those little knobs are raising the covers up and down, up and down" (*On Fire*, 149). Yet he offers Yankee the wooden chain he's whittling, and he volunteers to babysit Charlie while she goes out to look for work. Sebestyen gives very subtle hints that Yankee and Tater are attracted to each other, paving the way for Yankee's comforting gestures at the end of the novel.

The criticism that Tater's conversion occurs all too quickly might be answered by a reminder that he has been tormented by his murder of Ben Sills throughout the novel. He says that his decision not to kill Mr. Stoker was based on the memory of "that other night." "Tonight—I wanted him to be right about me," he tells Sammy. It is easy to forget, in light of Tater's wicked deeds, that he is still an impressionable adolescent. Throughout his young life, he has only had Pap to emulate. It is conceivable that, given the situation he has been thrust into and the people whom he meets, he could change the course of his life. Tater may be disadvantaged, but he is not stupid: having tried the way of lawlessness, he opts for a more hopeful future. He is just beginning to see that there is another way, as he tells Yankee, "I'm sorry . . . I didn't understand" (*On Fire*, 206).

Though *On Fire* was conceived to tell the Haneys' story, Yankee is a powerful force in the novel. "I kept thinking of the three of them in a kind of triangle," Sebestyen says of Sammy, Tater, and Yankee. She adds, "She was very important. She wanted to succeed, and she could do it, in her own way. And she's going to see that Charlie has a life, too." Yankee's blend of intelligence, strength, compassion, and honesty makes her one of the stronger female heroines in young adult literature.

Traveling alone all night to a strange town in order to claim her sister's body is a courageous act for Yankee, who refuses to be intimidated by the sheriff or by Doll Unger, her sister's "employer." Smart enough to know that she should have been consulted about the funeral arrangements, she accepts the fact that the burial has already been planned and goes along to the funeral service. But as the preacher speaks, Yankee is outraged at his insinuation that Nellie will burn in hell for her "wretched life." Refusing to listen to his hateful words, she runs from the service, convinced that her sister was a good person who loved her little boy. Later, after hearing Sammy's story, she barters with Doll Unger, letting the woman keep Nellie's clothes and jewelry if she promises to provide a home for Mrs. Haney and the children.

So many times in the novel, Yankee shows an inner strength and insight far beyond her fifteen years. Knowing the danger that Tater is in and aware that Sammy is determined to follow his brother—even if it means trying to jump a train to do so—Yankee makes it possible for him to accompany her as a paid passenger on the train to Pegler. Once there, she lets him live with her and Charlie in an old office-storeroom once used by her brother, Mick. Though she knows that the union will not allow her to live there, she continues to do so, hoping Mr. Eckert, the union boss, will not find out. When Eckert does come to the room and orders her out, she ignores him, vowing to stay until she is thrown out.

Yankee has a fanciful dream of settling the mine dispute by locking both sides together in a room and refusing them food, water, and sleep until they settle their dispute. She would have them exchange children, sending the bosses' children to the ash heaps in Back Town and the miners' kids to the comfortable homes of the mine bosses. This side of Yankee fascinates Sammy, who is impressed by her use of words like "motif" and her philosophical ruminations about people like the mine boss, Galen Stoker. Wanting to hate him for what happened to Mick, but remembering how he loved her sister, she says, "I know nobody's ever just one thing. We can't be. But I wish he was. If he could just be the enemy, it would be easier" (*On Fire*, 104).

Yankee's sensitivity to others' feelings is a mark of the compassion she shows throughout the novel. Besides making Charlie her own and taking Sammy in, she even lets Tater stay with them when he has nowhere else to go. Though his outward viciousness repulses her, she finds herself in his debt when he negotiates with Eckert to let her stay on for another month with a full coal bin. Unsure of her feelings toward him, and as hard as it is for her, she tries to apologize to Tater for her earlier insults. When she finds Mrs. Haney and the children alone and lost at the train station and takes them in, too, she does so without a thought for the little food and limited space they have. It is significant that Yankee is the one to comfort Tater in his torment at the end of the novel, since she is responsible for reuniting the family. As one reviewer says, "We hope Sebestyen will give her a novel of her own; she is unforgettable, the epitome of charity."[5]

Minor Characters

Though Sammy, Tater, and Yankee are the most fully developed characters in the novel, Sebestyen uses minor characters effectively in their development. Galen Stoker, for example, is more than the hard-hearted, money-grubbing mine boss. His contact with Sammy and Tater, on separate occasions, shows him as a thoughtful man with mixed feelings about the rancor that exists between the union and management, and as a sensitive man who has deep feelings for the people he loves. When Sammy first encounters Stoker, he is saying good-bye to his little girl, as she waves to him from the front porch of their big house. "I love you, Papa," she calls. "I love you, too, pet," he answers (*On Fire*, 163). Though Sammy is upset at finding out that this rich mine boss whom he wants to hate is a loving father, he is touched by the emotion between father and daughter. "He hadn't known people shouted words like that publicly" (*On Fire*, 163). Later, when he warns Stoker that Tater is trying to kill him, they get into a conversation about Yankee and her family. Stoker is visibly touched when Sammy mentions Nell, as Sammy observes: "He took off one glove and slowly pressed his forehead with his fingers as if he could smooth something aching behind the bone" (*On Fire*, 194). Sammy is reminded of Yankee's comment that nobody is just one thing.

Tater, too, is affected by Stoker's character. When the man asks Tater why he didn't shoot him when he had the chance,

Tater replies, "I rather use you. . . . I want a job" (*On Fire*, 197). Stoker is scornful, calling him "an opportunistic little rat. Ready to leave the sinking ship and go with the winners" (*On Fire*, 198). And when Sammy asks whether the mine bosses will win, Stoker replies, "Yes . . . and go on abusing its power until the union wins someday, and begins to abuse *its* power" (*On Fire*, 198). Nevertheless, he still entertains the idea of giving Tater a job, challenging Tater by telling him that he would have to work with a black man, Bledsoe. After thinking about it, Tater agrees, giving Stoker a deadline, noon the next day, to make up his mind or risk harm coming to him and his family. In spite of the threat, which he takes seriously, Stoker makes it clear that *he* will decide when to let Tater know, and he walks off, still in charge. It is then that Tater is roughed up by Bledsoe, to "start even," as the man puts it. Perhaps this is Ben Sills's revenge, wrought by another black man, as the beaten Tater tells Bledsoe, "Beating me into the ground don't prove nothing about you. . . . I know when a man's better than me. I killed a man better than me" (*On Fire*, 201).

Tater's speculation that his father may have hung himself as retribution for Ben Sills's death is one illustration of the effect his father has on his growth in the story. This hunch is not as far-fetched as it may at first seem, for Sebestyen wants us to wonder about Henry Haney. At the end of *Words by Heart*, we saw him picking the Sills's cotton, and we are not at all sure of his motivation. Was he trying to steal it, or was he trying to atone for the murder by his son of Ben Sills? We also saw, through Lena's eyes, his proud demeanor whenever he rode his horse and his skills with the lariat, suggesting a time before the drinking began, a time when he was a different man, one with self-respect. Though he doesn't play a major role in *On Fire*, his influence on Tater is strong. Tater's disappointment and anger at Pap's failures is actually the catalyst for his escape from a life of poverty and crime. Perhaps seeing what Pap has become and measuring him against Ben Sills helps him to decide not to pull the trigger on Galen Stoker. It is ironic that Tater wonders whether Pap killed himself as a last effort to punish him by saddling him with the responsibilities of a family, for it is these responsibilities that test Tater's mettle and help him discover the person he wants to be. Mrs. Haney, too, for all her weaknesses, has faith in Tater: she tells him that he can succeed where his father failed.

Critical Reception

Although it is common in young adult literature for adult role models to be conspicuously absent—it allows young protagonists to be self-sufficient as they search for identity—this aspect of *On Fire* has served as a basis of criticism from some adult readers. This convention is often necessary, though. Sammy, Tater, and Yankee gradually develop their respective identities by making mistakes, suffering loss, and relying on each other for help. If adult characters help them only indirectly, and not always in overtly positive ways, the character development of these young people is strengthened as a result.

Reviews of *On Fire* were largely positive. The *Horn Book Magazine* observed that "Sebestyen is able to explore the irrationality and injustice which are the roots of prejudice, without condoning its practice."[6] *Publishers Weekly* pointed out that "By the beauty and absolute rightness of her prose, the author compels us to care deeply about every one of the people we realize are in desperate conflict with themselves" (75). *Booklist* described the novel as one with "a powerful punch [that] offers a good deal of drama targeting the human price of class struggle."[7]

Some critics, however, have found the characters of Yankee and Tater less than credible. One reviewer complained that "Yankee's own struggle to reconcile conviction and compassion involves lots of earnest talk, some of it unlikely given her time, age, and circumstances."[8] Of Tater, this reviewer says, "His redemption may have come a little too easily" (*Horn Book*, J-44). Marjorie Lewis lamented in *School Library Journal* that "the racism issue is not explored, and although Sammy is uncomfortable with Tater's attitude, he never verbalizes his discomfort" (Lewis, 100).

Some reviewers also commented on the close link between *On Fire* and *Words by Heart*. Lewis feels that "without reading *Words by Heart*, it may be hard to understand why Tater was not prosecuted and why his vocal, virulent hatred of blacks is so much a part of his life" (Lewis, 100). Likewise, Stephanie Loer, writing in the *Boston Sunday Globe*, wonders whether "without reading the first book, readers may have difficulty understanding that 16-year-old Tater's raging prejudice against black people is a product of his own self-contempt."[9] Sebestyen agrees. "I tell kids, 'Please read the first book,'" she says. "It gives [*On Fire*] more meaning. . . . I can't imagine how somebody just reading it cold could get nearly as much." She is the first to admit that the two novels are companion texts, and that the resolution of the second depends upon a knowledge of the conflicts in the first.

Some readers have also been disturbed by the racial and ethnic slurs uttered by certain characters in *On Fire*. Tater frequently refers to blacks as "jigs" and "niggers" and to Italians as "wops" and "dagos," language he has learned from his father. Sebestyen admits that she had difficulties with these words as she was writing the book: "I found it troubling," she says. "I thought, 'I can't get away with this. I don't want kids to think that I would say this.'" She goes on.

> I hoped readers would realize that I had to make the characters as honest as possible . . . and that it's partly Tater's physical and spiritual poverty that is making him say this, because he doesn't know any other way . . . to express his rage or his feeling that somebody else must be to blame for what he is and what he does. So I researched the expressions that actually were used at that time and let him use them.

Though *On Fire* was generally well received, it did not quite achieve the success of Sebestyen's earlier novels. As Melanie Kroupa points out, Sebestyen's decision to pick up where *Words by Heart* left off was a courageous act.[10] Tater Haney was a despicable character, and setting out to examine the forces that made him commit murder was a daunting task. If the novel did not sit too well with some readers, perhaps this is because Sebestyen was so successful in developing Tater's character in *Words by Heart* that no amount of circumstantial exploration could alter that character in the reader's mind. Whatever the reaction, though, Sebestyen did tell the Haneys' story, and she told it well.

7. *The Girl in the Box*

"How pared down can a book be? Can it have one character in one place, one setting with one sort of dominant mood, and one time space that's very short? How close can you get to the bare minimum?" These were the questions on Ouida Sebestyen's mind when she conceived *The Girl in the Box*, her fifth novel and a drastic departure from anything she had previously written.

A minimalist work in the truest sense, *The Girl in the Box* chronicles the experience of sixteen-year-old Jackie McGee, who has been mysteriously kidnapped and thrust into a windowless cellar, sealed by a heavy metal door. The abduction occurs as Jackie is running down the street after her best friend, April, with whom she has had an argument and to whom she is trying to return the portable typewriter and ream of paper they shared. Once the closest of friends, Jackie and April have grown apart because of their friendship with Zack, a handsome, fun-loving boy whom they had made a part of their circle. They did everything together and were an inseparable threesome. Totally trusting of April and Zack, Jackie learns that they have become romantically involved and have kept their relationship a secret from her; she feels foolish and betrayed, and the realization devastates her. In retaliation for their betrayal, Jackie destroys the vegetable garden the three of them had planted and nurtured, knocking over tomato plants and ripping out bean vines, an act symbolic of the shattered friendship.

All of these memories play through her mind as she tries to figure out why she has been kidnapped and how she might be rescued. Though the kidnapper has left her stale baked goods and a large jar of oily-tasting water, Jackie cannot see what she is eating and has no idea how long the food will last. Having no bathroom facilities, except for a shallow drain in the floor, she must improvise with the plastic bread wrappers and cardboard donut boxes.

The abduction takes place on a rainy Thursday night, and the novel focuses on the ensuing days of Jackie's captivity. Making use of the typewriter and paper, which her captor has thrown into the cellar with her, she types notes to her parents, the police, her English teacher, April, Zack, even her kidnapper, "mailing" some of them by dropping them through a small slit next to the steel door through which light seeps in, with the hope that someone might find at least one of them. Some of her writings are what she calls "TTM," Talking To Myself, and it is through these written explorations that Jackie comes to better understand herself, her family, her friends, and her life. Positioning her typewriter on the bottom cellar step and using her folded-up raincoat as a seat cushion, she types in the dark, hoping that her words are being printed on the paper as she feels the indentations made by the typewriter keys.

As the days and nights drag on with no sign of rescue, Jackie becomes weak and disoriented, frequently crying and sometimes slamming herself into the concrete in frustration and anger as she raves hysterically against her captor. Alternating with these periods of hysteria, though, are times when she is totally in control, thinking lucidly and planning what she will do when she is rescued. Refusing to give in to hopelessness and despair, Jackie fights valiantly to keep her mind alert and her hope alive, even in the face of death. As the novel comes to an end, she is expectant, trying to climb the steps on her knees, moving toward the light.

The Girl in the Box is such an unusual book that readers frequently question Sebestyen's motivation in writing it. Sebestyen explains how the spark of an idea caught fire one day as she was traveling and "passed a kind of semi-industrial part of town. There was some sort of very thick-walled building, no windows, maybe a little door, and I thought, 'somebody could be locked in there and nobody would know it for years. . . . How would it feel?'" This question, along with her curiosity about paring down a novel to the bare minimum, stimulated her to try something new. "I had never written a book in the first person," she says, "and I thought, 'If you're going to write a book in the first person, it should be natural in some way, not somebody's total recall. . . . It should be moment-by-moment.'" Thus was the idea for *The Girl in the Box* conceived. The protagonist would be writing as she was experiencing the events of the novel.

Sebestyen's idea for the slit of light that turned out to be Jackie's ray of hope came from a personal experience, too. "My son's darkroom didn't quite get fully black," she remembers. "So I'd go in there to get something and wouldn't turn on the light, knowing where the something was. I found that if I lined up just right, I could suddenly see this little streak of gold, and know the world was out there. I thought, 'How comforting that would be to somebody, to know the world was going on, the sun was still shining.'"

One of the most remarkable elements of *The Girl in the Box* is Sebestyen's narrative technique, which involves deliberate experimentation on her part. Her wish to capture a moment-by-moment experience by having the protagonist type letters to herself and to others results in a unique structure for the novel, one in which flashbacks often occur, illuminating what is happening in the present. Many of these flashbacks take place in Jackie's letters to Miss Flannery, her English teacher, a character Sebestyen named after Flannery O'Connor. (She was inspired by O'Connor's statement that "evil is not simply a problem to be solved, but a mystery to be endured."[1]) The story-within-a-story technique that Sebestyen employs advances the plot even as it fills in the gaps of Jackie's past experiences with April and Zack and with her parents.

Always interested in writing, Jackie heeds Miss Flannery's advice to write about what she knows, which is how Sebestyen provides us with information about Jackie—her age, her physical description, her family life, her friendships. Interestingly, though, Jackie writes to Miss Flannery only three times—each time including part of her "story"—but then begins to write the story on her own, no longer needing Miss Flannery as a crutch. At one point she interrupts her story to "interview" No-Face, her captor, when she thinks she hears a *tick, tick, tick* sound somewhere in the cellar. Convinced that she is mistaken, however, she continues the story without missing a beat. Relating the events of her relationship with April and Zack helps her make sense of what went wrong with their friendship. With periodic interruptions for letters to her parents, her old dog Gillenwater Goodboy, and herself, she ends her story with her father coming to get her at the lake after her argument with April and Zack. After that, she sometimes writes to no one in particular, which makes her alternating periods of disorientation and lucidity all the more striking.

Sebestyen's technique of having Jackie write to various people works effectively to develop her character. This is important, for Jackie interacts with no one, save the brief encounter with her kidnapper, after her capture. When she writes to her parents, we see two conflicting sides of her personality. On the one hand, she is a little girl who wants to be protected by her parents and to depend on them. "I sure could use you, Daddy," she says at one point. Later, she begs, "Find me, please. This is hard to take."[2] In one of her "Talking To Myself" entries, she remembers, when she was little, her father asking her whether she wanted to be carried or to walk like a big girl. "Carried now, Daddy," she says (*Girl*, 75). On the other hand, though, she is the protector, trying to ease her parents' fears about her, assuring them that she is all right. "I'm okay so don't worry," she tells them (*Girl*, 8). And later she pleads, "Please don't blame yourselves for any of this. Promise you won't" (*Girl*, 35). "I'm sorry you're going through this," she apologizes. "Seems like all I can do is cause you trouble" (*Girl*, 36–37).

When Jackie writes to Miss Flannery, we see her studious side—a girl who loves to read, who delights in language, who enjoys writing (very much like Sebestyen herself). In one of her letters to the teacher, Jackie compliments her on her teaching style. "All those great words!" she exclaims. "Mollycoddle. Transcend. Wretched. You didn't think I was listening, did you, those days I stared out the window?" (*Girl*, 53). And, of course, it is the letters to Miss Flannery that prompt Jackie to write the short story about her relationship with April and Zack.

Jackie's letters to the police reveal the no-nonsense side of her personality, while they serve to provide her physical description and the factual information necessary to our understanding of the events surrounding the kidnapping. She is careful in her explanations to the police, mentioning that the kidnapper had a knife and cautioning them not to tell her parents about it. Her second letter to the police is much shorter and much less cordial, however. "What's holding things up out there?" she asks. "What's the foul-up? . . . Where are you? Aren't you even trying? . . . Get on the ball, out there" (*Girl*, 68–69). As her patience wears thin, Jackie needs to take her frustration out on someone.

Early in the book, Jackie writes a letter to April, and late in the novel she writes to both April and Zack. Each time she reveals her anguish at the breakup of their friendship. "Why did you say I ruined people's lives?" she asks April. "How could I do that?"(*Girl*, 48). And to Zack she confesses, "It wasn't your fault that I made you more than you were" (*Girl*, 146), ending the letter with a request that reveals forgiveness: "Don't let April do all the hurting while you do all the running"(*Girl*, 148).

Perhaps the most telling letters of all, however, are those Jackie writes to herself, trying to make sense of her situation while examining her conscience about the short life she has lived. Here we see all aspects of her character: her vulnerability, her courage, her tenacity, her honesty, her compassion, her sense of humor. Constantly questioning, she tries desperately to figure out why she has been kidnapped and by whom. She considers every possible angle, from a stranger grabbing her on a dare, to a crazed drug addict out for money, to a disgruntled criminal mistaking her for April. She even wonders for a minute if April and Zack might have planned the abduction as a way of scaring her and getting even.

Through these letters we see Jackie run the gamut of emotion, screaming and crying in frustration, then calming down by reminiscing about her family and her childhood days with her beloved dog. At times she becomes introspective, regretting that she was such a "self-centered brat" and recalling with sadness that she was once ashamed of the fact that her father was an auto mechanic and her mother was a second-grade teacher. We see her become weak and dizzy, then force herself to snap out of it "by pounding out words, words, words." In one TTM Jackie calls herself a "trusting idiot," taking the blame for her abduction. She becomes quite hard on herself as she gradually comes to realize that she has relied on others too much in her life, stunting her own emotional growth in the process.

Though her experience in the dark underground room is horrific, it is, ironically, the instrument of change in Jackie, as she works through the emotions of disbelief, anger, denial, fear, and acceptance. At first, after being captured, she is bewildered and types to no one in particular. She thinks primarily of the events of the kidnapping, and of how she will survive until she is rescued. She takes inventory of the baked goods and the water, explores with her hands her dark surroundings, and complains about the dampness and the silence.

As she becomes more angry and frustrated, she has intermittent crying jags, yelling at her captor, "Okay, No-Face, you goofed. All this stuff to eat and drink—so where's the Porta-Potty? What about a mattress and a blanket? Get your act together, you weird bastard—this is ridiculous!" (Girl, 27). Still disbelieving, she asks, "How could a whole day pass, and nobody come for me?" (Girl, 33). Her anger fuels her determination to get out, as she types a list of things she will do first once she is rescued. After two full days in captivity, however, she begins to waver, and fear creeps in: "I don't know what to do," she types to herself. "Isn't anybody coming? Ever?" (Girl, 67).

About this time Jackie's mood swings become worse, as she alternates between hoping that she will still be found and fearing that her life is over. Now she spends more and more time thinking about the people she loves and about their influence on her life. "The loneliness hurts like a bruise," she says (*Girl*, 73). Becoming more introspective, in a later letter to herself, Jackie laments all the time she wasted complaining about silly things and failing to really see the beauty of life around her.

Trying hard not to focus on her own hunger, she thinks about people who are "REALLY starving, really month-after-month starving until they feel their bodies breaking down to let their hearts and brains and vital things have any nourishment that's left" (*Girl*, 120). She wishes she had read more, so that she would have more things to think about and to fill the emptiness. "I've thought about a lot of things here that I never took the time to think about before," she observes. "Maybe we ought to have compulsory kidnapping" (*Girl*, 121).

Further evidence of Jackie's evolution is her increased concentration on spirituality, as she wishes that her parents had told her more about God as she was growing up. She remembers with regret her embarrassment when her neighbors talked frequently about their faith in God and wishes that she had questioned them about it. As her time in captivity drags on and she becomes weaker and more disoriented, she pleads, "Oh, God, you know I want to live. I was just getting the hang of it" (*Girl*, 151). In a heartwrenching passage, through dry, wrenching sobs, she types:

> Dear God,
> I am very scared.
> I wish I could tell you how I feel without being so on guard. I mean, there's always that question looming, separating us. If you know about me, and love me, why is this happening?

And revealing a more mature Jackie, she adds, "Maybe you could ask me the same question" (*Girl*, 152).

Perhaps the strongest evidence of Jackie's maturation is her letter to No-Face, her captor, in which she thanks him for leaving her food and for not abusing her sexually. "I wanted you dead," she says; "now I take back what I thought. Dead stops all possibilities. . . . I wouldn't want anybody to live like this, in the dark. I think you already know about the dark" (*Girl*, 154). Her wish that he receive help rather than punishment reveals a different Jackie from the one who earlier could see only her own wants and needs, a Jackie who is becoming more aware of life's deeper meaning as she wonders, "If going on living gives us a chance to do better, how can I ask it for me and not ask it for you?" (*Girl*, 154).

Jackie's acceptance of her situation is evident in the letter she writes to April near the end of the novel. In spite of her recurring bouts of disorientation, the letter is remarkably clear and coherent, revealing an unmistakable maturity. She talks of her fear of change and of death, of her desire to be safe and secure, coming to the conclusion that "dying's not all that earth-shaking," since it happens every second to someone or something. "Changes are how we grow," she says (*Girl*, 158).

Major Themes

Sebestyen explores several themes in *The Girl in the Box*, one of which is indomitability of spirit. We need only to imagine ourselves in Jackie's situation to marvel at her zest for life and her remarkable courage. Throughout the letters that she writes runs a thread of hope, a conviction that life is too precious to give up easily and too promising to live carelessly.

Each time she becomes depressed or fearful, she reminds herself that she must keep typing in order to maintain her connection to the outside world. After two nights in captivity, she tells herself, "I am going to be out of here today. This day. I believe it. . ." (*Girl*, 44). Hope is evident in her whimsical acts of listing what she would like for breakfast the next day and deciding what she will do first after she is rescued. Though Jackie's "interview" with No-Face halfway through the book reveals mental confusion on her part, as he repeatedly calls her "April," she takes control again and continues her short story for Miss Flannery. Even toward the end of the novel, when she is dizzy and weak and has occasional bouts of hysteria, Jackie manages to rein herself in and type yet another letter reaffirming her love of life. Her spiritual strength grows stronger as her physical strength weakens, keeping alive the hope symbolized by the slit of light coming through the door.

Closely connected to this theme of spiritual indomitability is the power of trust, an idea that permeates the novel from beginning to end. When Jackie first meets April, she is so thrilled to have such a wonderful friend that she practically makes April the center of her world. She is content to let April star in the plays she writes and envies her friend's "full life," even though she knows that April is sometimes lonely and insecure. She relies on her friend for happiness, assuming that April will always be there for her. The same thing happens when she and April befriend Zack: Jackie revels in their closeness, trusting her friends so completely that she fails to notice the meaningful looks that pass between the other two. She even resists thinking about the kiss she sees them steal in the dark.

Though Jackie gives her characters fictitious names in the story she writes for Miss Flannery, it's obvious that "Amy," "Lynn," and "Josh" are April, Jackie, and Zack. In one scene, when Josh asks Amy and Lynn what they like best about each other and why they became friends, Amy replies, "She was trusting" (*Girl*, 116). Soon after, when they discuss the trip around the world that they had planned, which now seems unlikely to happen, Josh smiles condescendingly and tells Lynn, "We're going to do it. Trust us" (*Girl*, 117). The innocent trust that Jackie places in her friends contributes to the hurt she experiences when they prove unworthy, unkindly hiding their relationship from her and making her feel left out. When she learns that April has been using that trust to lie to her father about her whereabouts, Jackie feels betrayed and confused, and she later berates herself for picking two actors as her best friends.

The most significant manifestation of trust, however, occurs at the end of the novel. Just when Jackie's situation seems most hopeless, when she has written a good-bye letter to her parents, she reaches within herself and regains control. "I'm in charge here," she says. "You can't finish me off until I say so"(*Girl*, 164). Thinking about all the wonderful things in the world, she exclaims, "I trust you, life," retrieving the hope that seemed to be slipping away and reaffirming her faith in her own ability to trust. To young readers who question her about the ending of the novel, Sebestyen replies, "Remember, I've already let the girl say all that really matters, there on the next to the last page. She says, "I trust you, life" ("Balancing the Books," 43).

Indeed, "life" is a dominant force in this novel, not only in Jackie's determination to survive, but also in the means she uses to assure that survival. Reflecting Sebestyen's own love of words, Jackie thinks about the French writer Miss Flannery had told her class about, wondering if "he was sort of unraveling himself like a sweater until he was all gone—but in his place was this pile of words with his life in them" (*Girl*, 120). Words are her pulse, as she frequently says in her letters to herself. Each time she begins to lose control, she reaches for words, pounding them out on the typewriter, resurrecting her spirit with their power. Even if she doesn't survive, Jackie has assured that she will live on through the words she has written to others.

The power of words is also evident in its subtle effect on Jackie as the novel progresses. Though she writes to survive, to communicate with the outside world, she also writes to understand herself, to make sense of the life she has led. Though she is not aware of this at first, the reader can see that she is working through her frustrations by writing about them, as she gradually comes to understand her feelings toward her family and friends—even toward her kidnapper—through her letters. Most important, though, she grows increasingly aware of her own life's meaning, enabling her to face whatever is in store without fear. This is the powerful message of the novel—that life is to be savored, that the spirit prevails, that hope transcends fear.

Evolution of the Novel

Though *The Girl in the Box* seems so well planned and well executed, Sebestyen admits it was a very difficult book to write. Three years in the making, the novel underwent several revisions that were sometimes painful for the author. In early drafts of the book the protagonist's name was Lundy, and the scene of her captivity was an elevator in an old, abandoned building. Zack was a more disturbed individual who ended up committing suicide after the breakup of the friendship. Concerned about the credibility of certain aspects of the plot, Melanie Kroupa, Sebestyen's editor at Little, Brown, encouraged her to keep working on the manuscript. Sebestyen revised and revised, rewriting various parts of the story and eventually changing the main character's name to Jackie and the setting to an underground cellar. She did, however, insist on leaving the ending of the book intact, in spite of concerns that it might be too frightening for adolescents. Says Sebestyen:

> *The Girl in the Box* was a bugaboo of a book to write, and a hard one to explain to anyone—even after they've read it! It isn't a crime story, but it is a mystery story, because it brings the main character and the reader nose to nose with some ultimate, perplexing and maybe unanswerable questions about life, and death, and why. . . . And it's scary, in ways beyond its surface plot, because it's saying we're on our own—no one else is responsible for our happiness or the smallness or largeness or quality of our lives. ("Balancing the Books," 43)

The seemingly grim ending is one element of the novel that bothers some readers, along with the credibility of the kidnapping and the coincidence of Jackie's having a typewriter and paper at her disposal in the cellar. As far as the ending is concerned, Sebestyen sincerely believes that Jackie survives. "She would have been found," she insists. "She just had too much hope and life in her. Even if you can't literally see her walk up the steps, you have a sense that she's larger and stronger." Many young readers write to ask her what happened to Jackie, convinced that she dies at the end of the book. Sebestyen replies, "You get to choose. What do you think? In your view of life would she survive? Or do you think it's hopeless?" She laments that young people are so used to having everything explained to them that they are shocked at open-ended stories, either unwilling or unable to decide for themselves what happens. By nudging them toward a deeper exploration of the novel, Sebestyen encourages young readers to examine their assumptions about life—and death.

An interesting anecdote concerning the ending of *The Girl in the Box* involves the words "The End" on the book's final page. They were unintentional and totally unrelated to the story. An earlier revision of the book had been sent to a publisher with the last pages missing, and the seemingly unsatisfactory ending almost caused the book to be rejected; fortunately, the missing pages were found, and the publisher agreed to take the novel. As a result, Sebestyen wrote "The End" on the last page of the final revision, to prevent any confusion about where the novel ended. The publisher, though, interpreted the words as part of the manuscript rather than as an explanatory note and they were included in the book, much to the author's chagrin. "It makes all the difference!" she exclaims. "Jackie wouldn't say that in a million years! It just changes the whole tone." Even though Sebestyen struck out the words on the galleys, they still appeared in print. "It's just a technical thing that got past," she says resignedly. Obviously, there's no way of knowing how much the words may have influenced readers' interpretations of the story's outcome.

Events leading to this outcome have been questioned by some readers, who feel that Jackie's kidnapping and captivity are too farfetched. Though Sebestyen has developed a logical explanation for Jackie's having the typewriter and paper with her, and for the kidnapper's throwing them into the cellar with his victim, skeptics feel that this aspect of the story is too contrived. "She has a jug of water, some packages of pastries, and . . . a ream of typing paper and a typewriter that she was carrying when abducted. It's an absolutely ludicrous premise, but a sensational appeal," writes one reviewer.[3] "The unreality of the premise produces a book that is not as strong as most of Sebestyen's others," charges another critic.[4] But those who question the credibility of the events surrounding the kidnapping itself might remember the abduction in December 1992 of ten-year-old Katie Beers on Bay

Shore, Long Island. The little girl was held captive in an underground chamber for sixteen days and was found only because her captor led police to the site. Katie lived on junk food, in a room that had neither light nor running water. She had no bathroom facilities, relieving herself in a box or on her bedclothes.[5] In fact, Sebestyen tells of a letter from a talk show notifying her that they were doing a segment about people who were locked up in their houses, and asking her if they might mention her book. "I had to call them and say, 'It's fiction, sorry,'" she says.

Though some critics were skeptical about *The Girl in the Box*, many were positive in their reviews of the book. Audrey Eaglen writes in *School Library Journal*, "Jackie must come to terms with her life and her imminent death. That she does so with incredible courage and grace is what makes *The Girl in the Box* transcend both the YA 'problem novel' genre and the horror genre. . . ."[6] *Horn Book Magazine* calls the novel "brilliant in the integrity of both its plot and the characterization of Jackie. . . . [Her] life and perhaps her death . . . sing a hymn to human goodness and dignity and a soaring tribute to one girl's courage."[7] Similarly, *Publishers Weekly* points out, "The power of Sebestyen's writing lies in the simplicity with which she delineates the intellectual and emotional processes of a girl in a box. The author has put herself in that box; this is a tightly focused writing exercise that is also a brilliant piece of suspense."[8] Anna Vaux, in the *Times Literary Supplement*, comments, "Ouida Sebestyen has written a strong book with some bleak moments."[9] One reviewer even speculates that Sebestyen deliberately evokes Robert Cormier's *I Am the Cheese*, which is also "a portrait of a teenager trapped by mysterious circumstances," in a work that "should make a provocative comparison to Cormier's book for years to come."[10] Though Sebestyen asserts that the similarity is not intentional, she admits to seeing how readers might draw comparisons between the two novels.

In their review for the *Journal of Reading*, Robert Small and Susan Murphy predict that *The Girl in the Box* "is a book that readers will either love or hate," adding, "and that is perhaps a sign of an important literary work." They go on to speculate that the painful ending, where no catharsis has occurred, may leave readers feeling cheated.[11] A review in *English Journal* is ambivalent about the book: Elizabeth Belden and Judith Beckman write, "We struggled over whether to recommend this book, and if so, how to review it. . . . We are stunned and bewildered by this story."[12] Though they are fascinated by the function of Jackie's writing in the story, they suggest that teachers read the work carefully before recommending it to students, citing Jackie's traumatic experience and the book's devastating ending. In a later review for *English Journal*, however, Donald Gallo praises "the sensitivity of Sebestyen's writing. . . . It's an Anne Frank kind of book," he says, "only in total, companionless darkness, without a discernable reason for being there."[13]

Like all of Sebestyen's books, *The Girl in the Box* contains autobiographical elements. Though she was never held captive, she tells of a high-school friend to whom she was very close: "We'd invariably want the same sweater when it was the only one in the store," she says. "And always the same boy. Hurt feelings and lots of problems through our friendship, but as we mellowed we became ourselves enough to know we weren't this set." As mentioned earlier, many of Jackie's qualities are Sebestyen's, and, as *Publishers Weekly* pointed out, her characterization is stronger for it. She and Jackie are in that box together, and it is the infusion of her strength into Jackie that brings them both into the light.

8. Short Stories and Drama

The magic that Ouida Sebestyen weaves in her fiction is not confined to her novels. The several short stories and one play that she has written contain the same kinds of universal themes, substantive plots, and character development apparent in her longer works. Unlike many short stories written for young adults, in which adult characters are often one-dimensional and sometimes cast in a negative light, Sebestyen's works frequently portray adults as multifaceted individuals who contribute significantly to the growth of the young protagonists.

"Words by Heart"

Chief among these characters, of course, is Ben Sills, the saintly father of Lena Sills in "Words by Heart," a short story that eventually evolved into the award-winning novel of the same name. Written under the pseudonym "Igen Sebestyen," it was first published by *Ingenue* in December 1968. "I used 'Igen' as a pen name during a very low point of my life, because it's the Hungarian word for 'yes!'" she explains. "Then I realized that my own name was even more affirmative—it contains both a French and a Russian *yes*: Oui da."[1] Perhaps Sebestyen's self-affirmation was infused into the character of Ben Sills, whose positive influence brings Lena to the realization that rewards "don't prove you're somebody." The story ends with Ben explaining to Lena, "When you're somebody inside yourself, you don't need to be told."[2]

Ben's strength of character and its obvious effect on Lena create a powerful story that invites further exploration—so much so that when Melanie Kroupa, then an editor at Little, Brown, read it, she encouraged Sebestyen to expand it further. The short story, which comprises the first one and a half chapters of the novel, was incorporated with only two alterations. In the story, Lena accepts the prize of a boy's bow tie after she wins the scripture-reciting contest, vowing to give it to her own little boy someday. In the novel, however, she refuses to accept the prize, dropping it on the table, turning her back, and walking out the door, thus preparing us for her spunky behavior later in the book. The other change involves her biological mother in the story, who in the novel becomes her stepmother, Claudie, enabling Lena and Ben to forge a closer bond cemented by their mutual experience of loss. This bond proves both a blessing and a curse for Lena as she searches for her identity.

"Welcome"

Other positive adults appear in Sebestyen's short story "Welcome," this time as elderly women and a retarded man. When Tina, distressed by the breakup of her parents' marriage, is forced by her mother to visit two of her father's aunts, she finds two women who, despite being alone, reach out to others with love and understanding. When Mary insists on stopping to see them on her way to visit her parents in Texas, eighty-year-old Aunt Dessie and Aunt Noella welcome Tina and her mother Mary without question. "I've never forgotten how they took me into the family," she tells Tina. "No questions. No testing. Just welcome."[3] At first critical and resistant, upset at being reminded by her great-aunts that she looks like her father, Tina gradually lets the family love seep into her, as she listens to Aunt Dessie explain why she and Noella remain close, in spite of the fact that they're not blood relatives. Initially frightened and repulsed by her retarded cousin Arley's strange behavior, she observes how Noella looks after him, accepting his shortcomings and loving him unconditionally. When Tina apologizes for screaming at the sight of Arley making faces through the window, Noella is understanding: she remembers, "When Arley was little and I finally knew he was never going to be right, I screamed too. Screamed and screamed" ("Welcome," 55). When Aunt Dessie suggests that they visit Noella's husband's grave at the cemetery, Tina is surprised at her own willingness to go, even though her mother is reluctant, and it is here that she encounters Arley face-to-face. Seeing her mother break down and cry, knowing that there is no hope of saving her parents' marriage, she runs blindly through the weeds, trying to understand why families break apart. Shocked to see a hand reaching toward her from behind a gravestone, she realizes that it is Arley offering her a flower to ease her sorrow. "Don't cry," he whispers. "I'm nice." At first afraid, Tina sees, "He had my father's deep eyes. The family face. Mine" ("Welcome," 57). Arley's kindness touches her as she bursts into tears, pouring out the frustration and anger she feels. As the story ends, Tina realizes that families may rearrange themselves, sometimes causing sorrow and heartbreak, but love can ease the pain. Thanks to the influence of Dessie, Noella, and Arley, she is decidedly hopeful, feeling she can handle whatever comes her way.

"Playing God"

Sebestyen creates two more intriguing adult characters in her short story "Playing God." The story focuses on young Josh, who wants to run away from home because he feels misunderstood and neglected, and his girlfriend Laurel, who tries to convince him to stay. It takes an interesting turn when Josh finds a box full of abandoned puppies under a bridge; he decides to postpone his trip for a short time in order to give the puppies away to loving owners. Since Laurel is helping with a party for a local poet at the library, Josh ends up there after managing to give away only one dog. There he meets "old lady Snap Crackle Pop," as he calls her (her real name Grace Whipple Cox), the poet whom Laurel has nicknamed the "Gnome de Plume" because of her tiny, sturdy, round figure.

As Josh overhears one of his classmates interviewing the woman for the school newspaper, he listens to her philosophizing about negative comparisons. Asked why she entitled her latest book *The Second Highest Point in Beymer County*, the poet replies, "To make a statement. . . . We act as if second-best is second-rate. . . . Everything has worth for its own reasons. . . . God doesn't label blades of grass Grade A and Grade B."[4] Aware that she is "not even a tenth-rate poet," she says that she continues to write poetry for herself, to create "for the fun of it!" When Josh asks Laurel what the second-highest point in Beymer County is, he is struck by her whispered answer, "Throne of Kings." Both are touched, for they realize that the poet had coincidentally named her book for "their place," a lovely piece of land where they go to find solitude, and where they had shared their first kiss.

Their impression of the Gnome as a stuffy literary lady is destroyed forever when, just as she is ready to leave, she offers to take two of the puppies. Uncertain of whether she has ten or fifteen years left to properly raise the pups, she rationalizes, "Fate has sent them a guardian angel once already. . . . Fate can do it again, if I don't last long enough. And they'll have each other" ("Playing God," 97).

Though Josh is unaware of it at the time, his brief contact with the Gnome has eaten away at his resolve to leave home for selfish reasons; he begins to realize that perfection is elusive, and that life must be lived day by day. His decision to go home and try once more stems from a new resolve to make things work.

A second adult character in this story, one who plays an even smaller role than the Gnome de Plume but nevertheless looms large for Josh, is the scruffy homeless man who appears at the party, helping himself liberally to the refreshments. Telling the startled group that he literally "cut his teeth" on the works of Rudyard Kipling, he admires the puppies, finally offering to take one. When a reluctant Josh asks for assurance that the man has a home and that the pup will be cared for, the man writes his address on a napkin; Josh recognizes the street from his paper-route days and realizes that the address is actually a warehouse. "Check on your pup," the man says. "See if I don't do a commendable job on it." Josh thinks, "He's begging. It's rough by yourself" ("Playing God," 95). His compassion is aroused when the man selects the runt of the litter, promising to be gentle with it. "I had a belt taken to me too many times to ever lift my hand to another creature," he tells Josh ("Playing God," 95).

The similarities between the man and Josh are striking, if not evident at first. The man is alone, not necessarily by choice, crashing a party for food and seeking love and companionship from a puppy. Josh is on the brink of making a choice that will separate him from all the things that this man longs for—family, friends, security, love. The man is a throwaway, like the puppies, and just as Josh rescues the puppies, he also rescues the man.

Sebestyen's magic in this story has two lonely adults inadvertently helping a confused young man, who in turn inadvertently helps these same two adults through an act of kindness—one that has nothing to do with them. At the story's end, in Josh's conversation with his father, we see the result of this magic: Josh becomes receptive to hearing with his heart rather than his head.

"After the Wedding"

In addition to presenting positive adult characters in her stories, Sebestyen has a knack for developing male-female relationships between young adults that enable one person to provide emotional support for the other. Sometimes she accomplishes this in an unconventional manner. In her story "After the Wedding," for example, we see two young people in a relationship that has gone sour for one and become a source of frustration for the other. Rusty and Jolene have returned to his hometown for his sister's wedding; while Jolene tries hard to fit in with Rusty's family, he runs off from the reception without even telling her. Puzzled as to why he is acting so strangely, Jolene presses him for the reason, only to learn that he wants to end their relationship.

At first Rusty appears to be an inconsiderate clod, delighting in the fact that Jolene admires his "perfect body," all the while holding her at arm's length. Sebestyen tells us, "She feasted on his face as he sat up. Suddenly she ached for him to reach out and beckon her close. . . . Rusty's long heavy-lidded gaze made her toes tingle."[5] This negative impression is reinforced when Rusty tells her, "Probably the most beautiful happy memory I'll ever have in my life is the surprise on your face every time I disappoint you" ("Wedding," 207).

While Jolene waits for Rusty to shower before they go out to dinner, she remembers how she met him, giving readers the information necessary to making sense of Rusty's actions. It seems that Jolene is several years younger than he, and that she was drawn to him because he gave her the attention she craved after years of being neglected by her parents. It also becomes apparent that he has had several girlfriends before her, none of whom meant much to him.

Not until they face each other over dinner, and he remembers his reaction to his father's recent death, do we begin to see that there is some depth to Rusty. Returning to the cemetery the day after the funeral, he had been struck by seeing *his* name on the tombstone: he had been named after his father. He tells Jolene, "I stood there looking at my name, and I realized I'd been trying so hard not to turn out like him that I hadn't turned out like me either" ("Wedding," 210–11).

When Jolene tries to be sympathetic, explaining why she was attracted to him and why she has stayed in the relationship, he turns on her, making a scene in the restaurant and accusing her of using him to satisfy her needs. The reader shares in Jolene's confusion—unsure whether to sympathize with him or take pleasure in his pain—while she wonders what is at the root of Rusty's problem. It is probably safe to say that at this point sympathy is with Jolene.

A short time later, however, alone in their bedroom, Rusty begins to tell Jolene what is bothering him. "After the wedding I was lying here, thinking what it would be like to be a father.

With a family. A wife. Giving my daughter away in marriage." In reply, Jolene asks, "And it scared you? . . . Didn't it ever bother you, all those years, that you might make babies when all you meant to do was make out?" ("Wedding," 214). His answer is to tell her that their relationship is over, but his reason comes as a surprise:

> You don't know what I'm saying, do you? I'm trying to give you a chance to escape, for God's sake. Honey, you're cutting off all your options. . . . My God, Jolene, you're bright, you're brave, you ought to be fighting your way into college and planning a life for yourself. ("Wedding," 214)

Jolene is not convinced, though. Unable to deal with this sudden change in Rusty, she tries to find other reasons for his behavior—something his mother said, or maybe an old girlfriend in whom he is interested again. In desperation, she tries to tempt him with her body. When even that fails, she feels abandoned, wondering what she will do with the rest of her life. Her dependency becomes apparent, as does his wish to set her free—or be free of her. "I wanted what you could give me. And you wanted what I could give you. That's just all it was, hon," he rationalizes. But the final question that Jolene asks can also be asked by readers: "How will I ever know if you're tired of me and lying about it, or if you really care about me more than anybody?" Rusty's reply gives no satisfaction, as he says, "You won't know, hon" ("Wedding," 216).

Though Rusty's final act is to pull Jolene to her feet, then slide his fingers free of hers, Sebestyen leaves us with just that little doubt about Rusty's motivation—a technique that she uses, with variation, in several of her works. She likes to make readers think and wonder. A pessimistic reading will label Rusty as a lying manipulator who will go on to other hurtful relationships. An optimistic reading will give Rusty credit for helping Jolene achieve independence while trying to take control of his own life. Either way, Jolene wins, helped along either inadvertently or intentionally by Rusty.

Holding Out

Another interesting young couple appears in Sebestyen's one published play, *Holding Out*. Curtis and Valerie, both sixteen, have traveled from California to Oregon in his father's pickup truck on a whim, namely, Valerie's hope that her father, who is divorced from her mother, will take her in. He refuses, which angers Valerie, but vowing not to go back to living with a mother whom she feels does not love her, she wants to run away. Curtis, the more sensible of the two, tries to make Valerie think about what she is doing and why her father might not have been able to take her in.

Again we have a situation where people use each other, as Curtis accuses Valerie of "coming on" to him and "working him over" until he was "ga-ga-gooey enough to steal a truck and head off [in] any direction [she] pointed to."[6] Incensed by his accusation, she tells him:

> Don't try blaming me for that part of it. You wanted to run as bad as I did. You didn't like the way you were living any more than I did. . . . You've been this nice quiet decent kid with the good grades—forever! You never had a problem because you never made a wave. Curtis—you needed to make a *wave*. A number nine wave, to see if it was going to drown you or if you could ride it in. ("Holding Out," 258–59)

Admitting that she did use him, she points out, "You used me, too. To test yourself. Am I right?" Curtis realizes that he too is guilty and tells her, "Sure. I guess it bothered me. I guess I thought about it, when my folks started planning my life for me, or things like that" ("Holding Out," 259).

Unlike Jolene and Rusty, however, Valerie and Curtis are on a more equal footing in their relationship and more honest in their dealings with each other. When they stop at a campground, Valerie notices that Curtis has brought only one sleeping bag. "Were you making big plans for us?" she asks. At first he denies it, but finally he admits, "Okay. It occurred to me. Just wrap up in it. Things turned out different. Okay?" ("Holding Out," 264).

The honesty and vulnerability that they share enable these two young people to help each other to understand themselves.

Yet the relationship between Valerie and Curtis is only one layer of this play. Sebestyen deepens the story by adding a second layer, a play-within-a-play in the background, in which a group of Modoc Indians reenact parts of the tribe's history. Curtis, who has been reading about the subject in his National Park Service guidebook, tells a disinterested Valerie about the seige in which sixty Modocs held off the U.S. Army for months in an effort to protect their land:

> But the white settlers wanted it, and got the government to send the Modocs to live on a reservation with another tribe they didn't like. So they ran away, and when the Army ordered them back, they refused, and gathered up their people here in the lava beds to hold out. ("Holding Out," 252–53)

As the shadowy figures continue to reenact scenes in the background, Valerie gradually becomes more interested and begins to ask Curtis about the Modocs. As the play shifts back and forth between the dialogue of Curtis and Valerie and the Modoc scenes, there seems to be no obvious parallel. However, the Modocs begin to reenact a scene in which rival leaders have argued and the loser kneels, beaten, his head bowed. A shaman appears with a medicine stick decorated with feathers, beads, and charms, and he plants it on a rocky ridge. Soon after, Curtis tells Valerie about the stick, which the guidebook says was supposed to give the Indians victory but had not. As they talk and Valerie starts to cry, feeling that her situation is hopeless, Curtis tells her that she must "hold out" until things get better. Comparing her to the Modocs, he points out that even though the Indians were not victorious, the fact that they made the effort is important. Wanting to think about what Curtis has said, Valerie leaves to walk the trail for a while. Left alone, Curtis sets about his work:

> With the sleeping bag's broken cord he ties together Valerie's feather, the pop can, and his booklet, and attaches the cord to the stick he used on his hike. He props the stick up on the table

with a pile of rocks, and slowly hangs Valerie's earring with the other charms. ("Holding Out," 270)

As the play ends with a dwindling line of Indians passing in the shadowy background, two sentries "glance back at the two medicine sticks standing bravely in the only light that is left" ("Holding Out," 271).

Sebestyen's effective juxtaposition of historical and present-day events adds to the play's sophistication, giving readers and actors plenty of room for interpretation in the performance of this one-act drama. The play's title, *Holding Out*, is also its theme—one that Sebestyen brings out in other works as well, and one that sends an important message to young people about courage and strength of character.

It is surprising that Ouida Sebestyen has written only one play, since as a child, and later as a young adult, she so loved writing scripts and "dressing up" for plays. As Donald Gallo points out in his book *Center Stage*:

> After high school she and a friend tried to start a little theater group in their staid West Texas hometown, "with disastrous but hilarious results—a comedy in itself." Later they both wangled jobs backstage at the University of Colorado's Shakespeare Festival, and for several summers they "padded Falstaffs, cloaked kings, and hooked handsome Romeos into their doublets."[7]

Perhaps *Holding Out* will be the first of many plays she will write, sharing her talent with a young adult audience who might be inspired to write plays of their own.

"I Gave My Son Away"

Though most of Sebestyen's short stories have been written with young adults in mind and published in anthologies marketed for adolescent readers, one early story that she wrote was published in *True Experience* magazine in 1971. Entitled "I Gave My Son

Away," it focuses on a husband and wife whose seven-year-old son Cloddy has been severely burned when a light plane crashes into his schoolroom and explodes. Having been designated "fire captain" for the second grade, he had taken his responsibilities seriously and stayed behind to free a classmate trapped under a fallen bookcase. The story is narrated by his father, Sam Keeler, who is agonizing not only over his son's condition but also over his inability to show his love for his son, to be close to him in the way he feels a father should be. Having substituted material things for love, he now finds that all he can give his son is payment of his medical bills—and even that is not possible on his meager income.

When his son dies, and the well-meaning townspeople offer to plan his funeral—free of charge—Sam is beside himself. Knowing that he can afford only a humble service at a country church, and also knowing that it would be his only way of giving love to Cloddy, he adamantly refuses the help, despite his wife's pleas to take the offer. When she reminds him that he did give his son something very important—life—he begins to relent, as the two of them come together, "giving life to Cloddy's love." The story ends with Sam feeling more secure and willing to acknowledge that his son is now "public property," that people need to be a part of him and what he stands for.

Conclusions

Because short stories are so brief and do not allow the kind of character development available in novels, the viewpoint from which the story is told is especially important. In "Welcome," for example, Sebestyen lets Tina tell the story of her experience with her parents' divorce and her encounter with her father's rather eccentric family. At first Tina's tone is cocky: she criticizes her mother, gripes about stopping to see a family she has never met, and makes fun of Dessie's appearance. Gradually, however, her tone softens as she tells of her sympathy for Aunt Noella and apologizes for screaming when she first saw Arley. In having

Tina narrate the story, Sebestyen allows us to feel her pain and the forces that begin to change her; as a result, the change becomes quite credible. Because of the limitations of first-person narration, we are not privy to the thoughts of others in the story; yet this is not a weakness, for the idea is to develop the character of Tina as much as possible within the constraints imposed by length.

In "Playing God" we have just the opposite situation. Though the story is about Josh, the point of view is "third-person omniscient"—a narrator who, not being a character, can see everything but innermost thoughts—which allows for a broader view of other significant characters. As mentioned earlier, the Gnome de Plume and the homeless man have stories of their own, which we must know about in order to appreciate fully their effect on Josh. By the end of the story, we are aware of their influence, though Josh himself is not.

Similarly, "After the Wedding" offers a more comprehensive perspective because it is told in the third person. The narrator, however, lets us see only Jolene's thoughts; Rusty is revealed primarily through his words and actions, which causes us to wonder just how much he can be trusted. Sebestyen allows us the latitude to decide for ourselves about Rusty's motivation.

Noticeable in all of Sebestyen's stories is an emphasis on the inherent goodness in people, even in the face of sorrow or emotional turmoil. Her short stories, as well as her novels and her one-act play, fly in the face of critics who charge that young adult literature is negative and often depressing, dealing only with social problems like suicide, divorce, child abuse, and teenage pregnancy. Certainly, her young people are not without problems—it would be unrealistic to portray them so, but she makes sure that they are also not without hope, that they find within themselves the strength to face those problems as well as the optimistic belief that they will find solutions.

9. Out of Nowhere

What is it like to be named after a motorcycle? Harley Nunn might say that it is not so great—not if it means being left alone to rust by the side of the road, with no one to bring you in out of the rain. And Harley should know. He was abandoned by his mother, Vernie, in the desert at the tender age of thirteen, after years of being moved from one foster home to another, while she chased after men who promised her elusive jobs in glamorous places.

Tired of listening to her empty promises and devious lies, Harley refuses to play a part in his mother's scheme to dupe her latest boyfriend into taking him along to Houston, where the man has promised her a job as a dancer. She has led her boyfriend to believe that they are taking Harley only as far as Arizona, where he is supposedly going to stay with his father, hoping that once they have gone that far, the man will let Harley travel the rest of the way. The truth is that the man Harley called "Daddy" has been dead two years, and that his mother has concocted this elaborate story, which falls to pieces when her boyfriend figures out that she is lying. Humiliated and disgusted, and knowing that he is not wanted, Harley refuses to travel any farther. Vernie feels guilty, but relieves herself of her burden anyway: she leaves him at a campground, instructing him to hitchhike back to California.

Enter May Woods, a sixty-eight-year-old woman who happens to have stopped for the night nearby, and who has witnessed the scene between Harley and the two adults. Shocked that a mother would abandon her own child this way, she feels sorry for Harley and shares her food with him, eventually coming back for him the next morning to ease her conscience. But Harley is not alone when she finds him. He has met a large black-and-white dog who has been abandoned by his owner. At first May refuses to take both the boy and the dog, but finally—assuming it's a temporary arrangement—she gives in and piles them into her old station wagon, Rosabella.

The rest of the novel takes place in and around May's old house, to which she has returned after many years of living in California. It seems that she too has been abandoned—by her husband of many years, who had been hiding another family all along, and who decided to return to them. Never content with simple arrangements, though, Sebestyen adds two more intriguing characters to the mix in order to make the dynamics even more interesting. Sixteen-year-old Singer (she has no last name) and cantakerous tenant Bill Bascomb, along with Bill's old yellow hound, Coo, complete the group. Together these four people and two animals learn to live with and in spite of each other, as they try to deal with internal conflicts while coping with the more immediate problems of sharing the same space.

In some ways reminiscent of *Far from Home*, with a thirteen-year-old male protagonist searching for a home, love and acceptance, *Out of Nowhere* explores what it means to love and be loved, to trust and be trusted. To this novel, though, Sebestyen adds a new element—the correspondences between humans and animals, the recognition that learning between the two is a back-and-forth rather than a top-down experience. Harley may be the protagonist here, but it is apparent from the start that the black-and-white dog, whom May names Ishmael, is equally important. "I wanted to write a book about a dog," says Sebestyen. "I love dogs and always had animals in my books on the side, so this one has a good main dog character."

When Harley first sees "Ish," as he calls him, the dog is in the back of a pickup truck. Shortly after, he sees the truck again, this time with the unwanted animal running desperately behind it in a futile effort to catch up. Soon after his own abandonment, Harley encounters the dog at night near the campground. He is frightened by its size and seeming ferocity, but, seeing the dog's own fear and trembling, he lets the animal stay with him as they take refuge from the rain in a roadside privy. The bond between boy and dog begins to develop, strengthening as Harley senses that Ish shares the hurt and unhappiness that he feels. May refers to them aptly as Flotsam and Jetsam, unwanted cargo washed up on the shore.

Characterization

Characterization has always been one of Sebestyen's strong suits, and in this, her sixth novel, she does not disappoint us. Perhaps her most striking character in *Out of Nowhere* is sixteen-year-old Singer, whom May and Harley first see atop the roof of May's old house, replacing shingles for Bill Bascomb. She tells them that she often comes to help Bill when he needs her, and she reveals that Bill is in the hospital, recuperating from an accident. Singer is not only spunky but smart as well—sometimes too smart for Harley. When he proudly tells her his dog's name is Ishmael, she beams, telling him it means "God hears." Taken aback and wanting to best her, Harley says that it has something to do with being exiled in the desert, to which Singer replies by telling him the biblical story of Hagar and her child Ishmael, who were banished to the desert. Her recollection that Hagar found water to keep her child from dying of thirst parallels the relationship between Harley and his dog throughout the story.

Like Harley, May, and Ish, Singer is alone, too. With her mother dead and her father confined to a veteran's hospital, she takes care of herself, occasionally doing odd jobs for neighbors. In spite of her situation, however, she is unbelievably cheerful, always smiling and finding the best in people—qualities that irritate May and bewilder Harley. Like Salty Yeager in *Far from Home*, she loves being up on the roof—up high, looking down at the world. She cherishes all forms of life, from the lowly spider that May impatiently washes down the drain to scruffy Bill Bascomb, whose slovenly ways she overlooks, for she sees only the man inside.

Indeed, she seems to be a fictional representation of Sebestyen herself—a lover of nature, animals, and life in general—at peace with herself and the world. Though May and Harley sometimes refer to Singer as "Miss Too-Good-to-Be-True," she is a likeable character whose ability to see all sides of an issue balances the extremes to which the others sometimes go. Perhaps this is Sebestyen's way of anticipating the criticism of those readers who find some of her characters too good. Her unflagging goodness calls to mind the character of Annie Garrett of *IOU's*, who also had autobiographical connections.

Singer's influence is widely felt, for there is not a character in the story that she doesn't touch. Harley quickly becomes attached to her, learning and drawing strength from her. She teaches him how to train Ish and how to love him. She impresses on him the importance of staying in school, of reading and learning as much as possible about everything. She helps him see the difference between love and love-making—love being unselfish and all-encompassing. Above all, she encourages him to believe in himself, to meet life head-on, confident of his ability to deal with it.

If it seems that Singer is incredibly wise, that wisdom is the force that moves the story along. Bill Bascomb is a good example: if we trust Singer, then we are willing to give Bill some latitude, even though he seems at first to be a hopeless slob. When we see what he has done to May's house, piling furniture and junk from floor to ceiling in every room, failing to clean anything, we see him through May's eyes. But through Singer's eyes we see him as a man who needs and gives companionship, who recognizes pain when he sees it and tries to ease it. He has befriended Singer because she needs a friend, and he is ready to do the same for Harley—even for May, if she will let him. Singer's positive way of looking at the world brings out the best in Bill, and this becomes apparent as the story evolves. We get the feeling that she has had the same effect on him as she has had on Harley.

In spite of her resistance, even May is touched by Singer. Though from the start she makes it plain that she is suspicious of the girl and annoyed by her unfailing cheerfulness, May does remember that Singer is a vegeterian when she shops and prepares meals—a considerate gesture to which she would never admit. Her hostility toward Singer stems more from her own insecurities than from her dislike of Singer as a person. Singer is kind to May, even in the face of insults, working hard to help her clean up the house, trying to nurse her injured hand when she cuts herself, even playing peacemaker in the ongoing battle between May and Bill. Yet it is not until Singer leaves that May has regrets, fingering the packet of seeds that the girl has left her as a parting gift, a gift of life for the future.

In spite of her inability to show affection to Singer, May is a good woman at heart. The fact that she takes in Harley and Ish early in the novel is evidence of this, even though she intends it as a temporary arrangement. Describing herself to Harley as "a weirdo running away from home," she explains how she changed the spelling of her name from "Mae" to "May," like the month, and how happy she was to marry Nolan Woods because her name then became May Woods. Like Singer, she resembles Sebestyen herself in her love of nature. Her eagerness to start a garden, and her determination to keep it going, mirror the author's penchant for cultivation and nurturing.

If May's soft side is not readily apparent in most of the novel, it's because she tries very hard to be tough, to prove to herself that she can survive without a husband. Feeling hurt and betrayed at having been deserted, she admits to having become someone unfamiliar; nevertheless, she is determined to take control of her life. This is why she is so adamant about cleaning up the mess that Bill Bascomb has left, and about ridding the house of his presence. Her obsession with cleanliness, as she orders Harley and Singer to scrub, scour, and paint, reflects her desire to start anew, with no ties to anyone or anything. It also explains her initial refusal to take Harley in permanently, to give him the home he longs for. Though she knows that he and she are very much alike in their sorrow at having been abandoned by someone they loved and trusted, she is uncertain of whether she can even take care of herself, let alone take care of a teenage boy.

May's inner conflict also helps explain her hostility toward Bill Bascomb. Aside from the fact that she can't abide his pack-rat mentality and slovenly housekeeping, she is also resentful of his claim on her house. Her childhood home is the only tangible possession she has left, a symbol of her potential independence, and Bill's presence presents a threat to her. Having spent the past thirty years as a dutiful wife, she doesn't need another man in her life determining her future. Her frequent confrontations with Bill stem from this fear and from her need to lash out at someone in order to ease her anger and frustration.

May is a classic case of the displaced older woman, alone and afraid, unsure of her ability to cope with the drastic change in her life. Her marriage produced no children, so she may see in Harley the son she never had. She is kind to him, which contrasts with her behavior toward Singer and Bill; she confides in Harley, telling him of her husband's betrayal and how it affected her. And though Harley does not know what to do with this confidence at first, he acts on his instinct to try and comfort May in his own awkward way.

From the very start, Harley sees May as a potential guardian, someone who can give him the home and security he needs and wants after having been treated as excess baggage for thirteen years. Sebestyen expertly portrays Harley as a naive, unschooled boy who wants to learn but feels very inadequate. He is hard on himself, frustrated at every mistake he makes that he "just didn't do things right." Yet he is a willing pupil, one who learns about life and love from May and Singer.

Likewise, Harley also learns from Bill. At first he notices only his clutter, but Harley begins to see that Bill knows where everything is, that he can put his finger on things at a moment's notice. Though his organizational system may be unconventional and unsightly, Bill maintains control of his belongings—until May comes along. And it is Bill who reveals to Harley that Ish is a pit bull, a revelation that frightens the boy, who remembers the stories he has heard about the ferocity of such dogs. When Bill patiently explains that the way the dogs are trained by their masters makes all the difference, Harley begins to understand the significance of the relationship between humans and animals. He learns his final lesson when Bill tells him he must decide whether or not to let the vet amputate Ish's leg, which was injured when he jumped from a truck in an effort to follow Harley. Realizing that no one can make the decision for him and feeling responsible for the situation, Harley agonizes over the thought of his dog suffering, but decides in favor of the amputation—a decision that marks a turning point in Harley's journey toward maturity.

One of Harley's biggest problems in the novel is his insecurity. Though he longs for someone to care for him, he feels awkward showing any kind of affection himself. An incident with Ish illustrates this clearly. When Harley and Singer take a break from their work to wander down to the creek with the dogs, Ish is obviously afraid of venturing into the water with them. After coaxing the dog several times, Harley becomes frustrated and gives up, obviously disappointed in Ish. Just as he turns his back to walk away, he hears the dog plop into the water and begin to swim toward him, willing to risk anything to please his master. Harley is touched, but doesn't know what to do when Ish reaches the shore. Conscious of Singer's cry to "love him up," Harley does not know how to do this; instead, he awkwardly pats the dog on the head. Aware that he "did it wrong," he is upset at himself for not being able to give Ish the affection he deserves. Though he is not aware of it at the time, Harley is behaving toward Ish in the same way his mother behaved toward him.

Soon after, another incident occurs that amazes and embarrasses Harley. As he and Singer talk about what real love means, she professes her love for him, and May, and Bill. Taken aback, Harley does not know how to respond, so he instinctively rejects her—until she reminds him that she is talking about caring, friendship, and "holding dear"—not the sexuality that he equates with the word "love." At the end of the novel, when Singer leaves, Harley wonders how he will manage without her; but he soon begins to realize that the love Singer left behind will always be with him—and with May and Bill as well. Because of Singer, Harley becomes more comfortable accepting and returning Ish's unconditional love. No longer just a "taker" who longs for someone to love him, he becomes "giver" who is willing to divide and share that love. We get the feeling that May and Bill will be recipients, too.

Though he is the last character to be introduced by Sebestyen, Bill Bascomb is an interesting addition to this story. At first he seems like the grizzly, stereotypical old coot who has lived by himself too long. A few years younger than May, he appears to be a loner who wants to remain that way. But then we learn that Singer has been his friend for quite a while, and we wonder why a lively sixteen-year-old would spend her time with a jaded old man. As the story unfolds, though, we see that there is much more to Bill than a cantankerous personality. He is smart, compassionate, and determined, and his presence in the story is significant. Like Singer, he inadvertently prompts both Harley and May to take a hard look at themselves, even though they do not always like what they see. He forces both of them to face up to their responsibilities—Harley's for Ish, and May's for herself and Harley. In the process, he becomes more mellow himself, developing a genuine affection for both of them. Though he tangles with May over possession of the house, he comes up with an idea to help her financially by converting the storage shed into a rental apartment. And when he sees that Harley has no money to pay the vet's bill for Ish's care, he offers to help, even selling his beloved old junkheap of a car with some of his other possessions and giving Harley half the money.

Any examination of the novel's characters must include Ish, since Sebestyen set out to write this story with the dog in mind. The fact that he is a pit bull, an animal feared and even hated by some, makes his devotion to Harley all the more interesting. Significant, too, is the fact that Harley became attached to the dog before he learned of his breeding. Had he known at their initial encounter at the campground, he may very well have run from the dog, never giving Ish the chance to prove the truth of Bill's words about the link between animals and their masters.

Through Ish, Sebestyen shows that animals, like people, are often stereotyped and misunderstood, needing only a chance to prove themselves. By creating the common ground of abandonment among Ish, Harley, and May, the author draws animal and human together in a circle of need that gradually strengthens into independence based on love and trust. Through his unwavering trust and devotion, Ish is the catalyst in providing this strength for both Harley and May.

The dog's name, Ishmael, is certainly significant, as are the names of others in this story. Singer's pointing out that the name means "God hears" provides the first clue that this animal will be more than a background pet in the novel. His name symbolizes a force that brings together four people and a dog who work little miracles on each other, a metaphysical view that harmonizes well with Sebestyen's down-to-earth plot and true-to-life characters.

Singer, too, bears a name worthy of note. The melody of life is her theme song, as she manifests her music in the hearts of others. Though, as May says, she seems at times too good to be true, her ability to always see the goodness in people is instrumental in enabling others to see the goodness in themselves. Her genuine desire to be helpful, her compassion for even the lowliest creatures, and her deep appreciation for the beauty in the world provide the lyrics to the song of life that she loves to sing. Once these lyrics are learned by others, she moves on, eager to sing her song in other places for other people.

More evidence that naming is important in Sebestyen's books comes with May Woods. Changing her name from "Mae" to "May," like the month, was an important step in her life. It is almost as if she knew what the future held. The month of May is a time of promise when trees blossom and flowers begin to bloom. May herself is like this. Dependent for most of her life on someone else, she begins to blossom at the age of sixty-eight, setting off alone to face her future. Though she is fearful and insecure, her resolve is strong and continues to grow, just like the plants she nurtures in her garden. In May the woods are full of budding life, just as May Woods gives life to seeds that have been dormant for many years. How fitting that Singer should give her a seed packet as a parting gift so that she may plant new growth and continue the cycle of life.

Ishmael, Singer, and May are lovely names that call to mind pleasant thoughts. Poor Harley, on the other hand, was named for a motorcycle because his mother said it was the easiest thing to do, since she did not know who his father was—and happened to be traveling with two motorcyclists at the time. Instead of God, or music, or nature, his name conjures up images of tatoos, chains, and black leather jackets. Even his last name—Nunn— brings to mind a zero, a nothing, indicative of how he feels about himself early in the novel. Even though he is not exactly happy with the name, Harley doesn't let it become a self-fulfilling prophecy. Determined to have a home and not be a wanderer like his mother, he debunks any stereotypes associated with his name—just as Ish contradicts Harley's preconceived notions about pit bulls.

Setting

As naming is closely tied to characterization in *Out of Nowhere*, so is the setting of the novel in close correspondence to the plot. When we first meet Harley, he is abandoned in the desert, apparently unloved and uncared for. The hot, dry landscape mirrors the dryness in Harley's soul, the disgust for his mother and her boyfriend and the anger at being abandoned in unfamiliar surroundings. Ish, too, is deserted here—fearful and apparently abused. And it is in the desert that Harley meets the abandoned May, frustrated and frightened as she makes her way to an uncertain future. The prevailing emotions at this point in the novel are overwhelmingly negative, as the three characters—fresh from their own misfortunes—size each other up and consider the risks of trust. Significant, too, is the parallel with the biblical story of Hagar and Ishmael, who also were abandoned in the desert. But there is a small oasis in this desert, the promise symbolized by the name May Woods.

As Harley and May travel out of the desert toward her old home, Singer comes into the picture, bringing with her a freshness and zest for life that will figuratively slake Harley's thirst. The incident at the creek with Ish marks a turning point for Harley, as he begins to give rein to his feelings, trying to love the dog in his awkward way, laughing and joking with Singer. The creek offers a baptism of sorts, the beginning of a new life for him and the dog. Throughout their time together at May's, Singer plants her own seeds of love and caring, which eventually parallel the garden that May plants and nurtures. As the story progresses and Singer's influence takes hold, the emphasis shifts from self-absorption and distrust on the part of Harley and May to selfless-ness and sharing. They are far from the desert now: abandon-ment has led them, along with Ish, to a home and family, to loving acceptance.

Themes

Out of Nowhere explores a theme that Sebestyen introduced ear-lier in *Far from Home*: the power and importance of extended family. But her "family" is not the conventional group that most people think of when they hear the word. Instead, it consists of a conglomeration of the most unlikely individuals thrown together by happenstance and forced to get along. Most significant is their effect on each other and the changes that result from their inter-action.

While in *Far from Home* we have two supposed "outsiders"— Salty and Mam—trying to break into the Buckley family circle, in *Out of Nowhere* we see four virtual strangers coming together under the most curious of circumstances to form a family under protest. At first May completely rejects the idea of taking Harley in permanently: she views Singer as a "mysterious little creature," is not at all sure she wants the burden of a dog, and cannot abide the thought of being anywhere near Bill Bascomb. Since the house belongs to May, the thought of this group living together under its roof seems remote at best. Yet Sebestyen manages to create a series of parallels that, while slightly contrived, effectively intertwine the lives of these four people and a dog. Their shared lone-liness is a powerful force in bringing them together, as is their natural inclination to goodness.

Because Harley has never experienced real maternal love, he is drawn to May, who represents the female influence missing in his life. Never having had siblings—or a real friend, for that mat-ter—he finds in Singer a companion near his age with whom he can communicate. Bill Bascomb becomes the male role model Harley sorely needs—someone to teach him responsibility and respect for life. And Ish, of course, is the catalyst for Harley's emotional growth throughout the novel, giving him a reason to be responsible and caring and showing him what it means to trust and to love.

May also has needs that are filled by the others. Though she is reluctant to form an attachment to Harley and seems to be annoyed by Singer, their youthful presence brings energy to her life—the children she never had. Because Harley's experience par-allels her own, she sees in him a mirror image of herself; if he is okay, then she is okay. Perhaps her dislike of Singer stems from her envy that this young woman is free and unfettered by conven-tion, while she spent her young womanhood bound in a stifling marriage. Perhaps she also comes to the realization that it's never too late to be like Singer. Bill, too, helps May to deal with this drastic change in her life. Though they argue frequently and are miles apart philosophically, Bill shows May a different kind of man from the husband with whom she lived for thirty years, a man who recognizes goodness and knows how to care. Her deci-sion to let him stay on reflects the "new May," no longer worried about failing and confident in her ability to begin a new life.

The last person to come into this unusual family, Bill Bascomb, is also enriched by the presence of the others. A loner for many years, he seems content to remain so but really comes into his own when his life is disrupted by these unusual people. Though Singer believes that she is helping Bill by coming to his place when he needs her, we suspect that Bill is also helping her by being a friend to a lonely girl. There seems to be an unspoken understanding between the two of them—a kind of warmth that glows at both ends. When Singer is ready to leave, Bill accepts her decision, commenting that she was there when they needed her most. May, too, gives Bill reason to start thinking of others rather than just himself. Though she is hostile and insulting to him, he tries to understand her abrasive behavior and even looks for a way to help her support herself financially. Not having had a woman in his life for a long time, he resists this change, but it becomes apparent that he has a soft spot in his heart for May, in spite of himself. This compassion extends to Harley, too, as Bill gradually begins to serve as a mentor to the boy, realizing that he has a lot to learn.

Most young adult novels deal with self-discovery and the emotional growth of the young protagonists. Ouida Sebestyen's books, however, are unique in that they also examine the lives of adults. Again, *Out of Nowhere* and *Far from Home* are similar in this respect. The adults in the novels are not just background figures who influence the growth of the protagonist; they are significant characters in their own right whose lives are complicated by factors unrelated to the main character. Sebestyen's treatment of these characters in her books adds an extra dimension to the works that transcends the stereotypical young adult problem novel.

Just as in *Far from Home* we watch the Buckleys and the McCaslins struggle with the adult problems of marriage and family, so in *Out of Nowhere* we see May Woods and Bill Bascomb wrestle with conflicts that have evolved throughout their lives. Though May is determined to become a liberated woman at sixty-eight, she is fearful and defensive about starting a new life. Without being heavy-handed about it, Sebestyen makes it clear that May has been a submissive wife all her adult life and that she is having difficulty adjusting to a solitary existence. That she is able, through her association with the others, to come to terms with some of her fears is testimony to the fact that learning and growing are not a function of age.

Bill, too, undergoes change in the novel. At first he seems hermitlike—self-centered and determined to have things his way. He's been alone so long that he has forgotten how to get along and compromise. We get the feeling that he has experienced his share of heartache, too. But a transformation takes place as the story evolves and Bill shows himself to be a much more likeable person. Unlike the change in May, however, Bill's conversion seems to happen a bit abruptly, and the reasons are not fully explored. Ish's accident and Harley's reaction are apparently the precipitating factors, but we don't learn enough about Bill's past to make clear sense of the change that takes place in him.

Nevertheless, Bill's presence adds richness to the novel and conveys the message that self-discovery can occur at any time in life. Like all of Sebestyen's other novels, *Out of Nowhere* celebrates the human spirit. It gives us a glimpse into the mind and heart of a novelist who lives what she believes and writes so that young people will believe it too.

Notes and References

1. A Loner, but Never Lonely

1. Ouida Sebestyen, "Family Matters," *The ALAN Review*, Spring 1984, 2; hereafter cited in text as "Family Matters."

2. Ouida Sebestyen, "How I Spent My Misspent Youth So Far," publicity material for Little, Brown Publishers, 3; hereafter cited in text as "Misspent Youth."

3. Lyn Littlefield Hoopes, "Novels of Ouida Sebestyen Share Thread of Good," *Christian Science Monitor*, Friday, 3 May 1985, n.p.

2. Making Magic

1. Ouida Sebestyen, "Balancing the Books," *Work and Play in Children's Literature*, selected papers from the International Conference of the Children's Literature Association, eds. Susan R. Gannon and Ruth Anne Thompson, June 1990, 41; hereafter cited in text as "Balancing the Books."

3. *Words by Heart*

1. Ouida Sebestyen, *Words by Heart* (Boston: Little, Brown, 1968, 1979), 134; hereafter cited in text as *Heart*.

2. Jean F. Mercier, "Story Behind the Book: *Words by Heart*," *Publishers Weekly*, 28 May 1979, 40; hereafter cited in text.

3. Kristin Hunter, "Blurred View of Black Childhood," *The Washington Post*, 10 June 1979, E3; hereafter cited in text.

4. Quoted in Rudine Sims, "*Words by Heart*: A Black Perspective," *Interracial Books for Children Bulletin* 11.7, 1980, 15; hereafter cited in text.

5. Carol Gilligan, Nona P. Lyons, and Trudy B. Hanmer, *Making Connections: The Relational Worlds of Adolescent Girls at Emma Willard School* (Cambridge: Harvard University Press, 1990), Preface; hereafter cited in text.

6. Nikki Giovanni, Letter to Melanie Kroupa, 22 July 1979.

7. James Brewbaker, "Are You There, Margaret? It's Me, God—Religious Contexts in Recent Adolescent Literature," *English Journal* 72.5, September 1983, 86.

8. Fay Wilson Beach and Glyger G. Beach, "*Words by Heart*: An Analysis of Its Theology," *Interracial Books for Children Bulletin* 11.7, 1980, 16; hereafter cited in text.

9. Kenneth L. Donelson and Alleen Pace Nilsen, *Literature for Today's Young Adults*, 3d ed. (Glenview, IL: Scott, Foresman, 1989), 434; hereafter cited in text.

4. *Far from Home*

1. Ouida Sebestyen, *Far from Home* (Boston: Little, Brown, 1980), 3; hereafter cited in text as *Home*.

2. "*Far from Home*." *Horn Book* 57.1 (February 1981), 60–61.

3. "*Far from Home*," *Booklist* 77, September 1980, 120.

4. James Holmstrand, "Novels of the Heart," *The Bloomsburg Review*, July/August 1981, 7 and 20.

5. Patricia Lee Gauch, "*Far from Home*," *New York Times Book Review*, 18 January 1981, 31.

6. "*Far from Home*," *Kirkus Reviews*, 15 December 1980, advance review.

7. "*Far from Home*," *Booklist* 77, September 1980, 111.

8. "*Far from Home*," *Bulletin of the Center for Children's Books* 34, September 1980, 21.

5. *IOU's*

1. Ouida Sebestyen, *IOU's* (Boston: Little, Brown, 1982), 20; hereafter cited in text as *IOU's*.

2. Melanie Kroupa, Memo to John Keller, 5 November 1981.

3. Dick Abrahamson and Betty Carter, "Positive Young Adult Novels," *English Journal* 71.8, December 1982, 66.

4. Arielle North, "Of Love and Dependence," *St. Louis Post Dispatch*, 6 June 1982, n.p.

5. Colby Rodowsky, "'Tis the Season for Sand Between the Pages," *Baltimore Sun*, 25 July 1982, D4.

6. Melanie Kroupa, Letter to Ouida Sebestyen, 1 September 1981.

7. Ouida Sebestyen, Letter to Melanie Kroupa, 25 September 1981.

8. "*IOU's*," *Kirkus Reviews* 50.8, 15 April 1982, 496–97.

9. "*IOU's*," *Horn Book*, August 1982, 418.

6. *On Fire*

1. Tom DeMers, "The Great Colorado Coal Strike," *The Sunday Camera Magazine*, 22 April 1984, 12–13.

2. Marjorie Lewis, "*On Fire*," *School Library Journal* 31, April 1985, 100; hereafter cited in text.

3. Ouida Sebestyen, *On Fire* (Boston: Little, Brown, 1985), 80; hereafter cited in text as *On Fire*.

4. "*On Fire*," *Bulletin of the Center for Children's Books* 39–40, 1985, 17.

5. "*On Fire*," *Publishers Weekly* 227, June 1985, 75; hereafter cited in text.

6. "*On Fire*," *Horn Book* 61, July/August 1985, 459.

7. "*On Fire*," *Booklist*, 15 May 1985, 1338.

8. "*On Fire*," *Kirkus Reviews* 53, 15 May 1985, J-44.

9. Stephanie Loer, "*On Fire*," *The Boston Sunday Globe*, 15 September 1985, 100.

10. Melanie Kroupa, Letter to Jim Trelease, 12 February 1985.

7. *The Girl in the Box*

1. Ouida Sebestyen, "Balancing the Books," *Work and Play in Children's Literature*, selected papers from the 1990 International Conference of the Children's Literature Association, eds. Susan R. Gannon and Ruth Anne Thompson (June 1990) 43; hereafter cited in text.

2. Ouida Sebestyen, *The Girl in the Box* (Boston: Little, Brown, 1988), 65; hereafter cited in text as *Girl*.

3. "*The Girl in the Box*," *Bulletin of the Center for Children's Books* 42 (1988), 53.

4. "*The Girl in the Box*," *School Library Journal* 35 (October 1988), 164.

5. Diana Jean Schemo, "A Lonely Girl Looks for Friendship and Finds Terror," *New York Times*, 17 January 1993, 29, 34.

6. Audrey B. Eaglen, "In the YA Corner," *School Library Journal* 35, June 1989, 58.

7. "*The Girl in the Box*," *Horn Book* 64 (November/December 1988), 791.

8. "*The Girl in the Box*," *Publishers Weekly* 234, 9 September 1988, 135.

9. Anna Vaux, "Why Are We Here?" *Times Literary Supplement*, 3 November 1989, 1219.

10. "*The Girl in the Box*," *Kirkus Reviews* 56, 1 September 1988, 1328.

124 NOTES AND REFERENCES

11. Robert Small and Susan Murphy, "Books for Adolescents," *Journal of Reading* 33, January 1990, 312.

12. Elizabeth A. Belden and Judith M. Beckman, "Heroes and Victims Meet Adventure," *English Journal* 78.6, October 1989, 81–82.

13. Donald Gallo, *"The Girl in the Box," English Journal* 79.5, September 1991, 96.

8. Short Stories and Drama

1. This explanation was handwritten by Sebestyen on the back of the table of contents of the *Ingenue* issue in which the story appeared. The page is part of the Kerlan Collection at the University of Minnesota's Walter Library.

2. Igen Sebestyen, "Words by Heart," *Ingenue*, December 1968, 72.

3. Ouida Sebestyen, "Welcome," in *Sixteen Short Stories by Outstanding Writers for Young Adults*, ed. Donald R. Gallo (New York: Dell, 1984), 48; hereafter cited in text as "Welcome."

4. Ouida Sebestyen, "Playing God," in *Visions: Nineteen Short Stories by Outstanding Writers for Young Adults*, ed. Donald R. Gallo (New York: Dell, 1987), 93–94; hereafter cited in text as "Playing God."

5. Ouida Sebestyen, "After the Wedding," in *Connections: Short Stories by Outstanding Writers for Young Adults*, ed. Donald R. Gallo (New York: Dell, 1989), 207; hereafter cited in text as "Wedding."

6. Ouida Sebestyen, "Holding Out," in *Center Stage: One-Act Plays for Teenage Readers and Actors*, ed. Donald R. Gallo (New York: Harper and Row, 1990), 258; hereafter cited in text as "Holding Out."

7. Donald R. Gallo, ed., *Center Stage*, 272.

Selected Bibliography

Primary Works

Novels

Far from Home. Boston: Little, Brown, 1980.
The Girl in the Box. Boston. Little, Brown, 1988.
IOU's. Boston: Little, Brown, 1982.
On Fire. Boston: Little, Brown, 1985.
Out of Nowhere. New York: Orchard Books, 1994.
Words by Heart. Boston: Little, Brown, 1979.

Unpublished Novel

The Dwelling Place

Short Stories

"After the Wedding." *Connections: Short Stories by Outstanding Writers for Young Adults*, ed. Donald R. Gallo. New York: Dell, 1989.
"Children Are a Blessing." *Everywoman* (Canada), 1950; *Mother and Home* (England), 1951.
"Playing God." *Visions: Nineteen Short Stories by Outstanding Writers for Young Adults*, ed. Donald R. Gallo. New York: Dell, 1987.
"Welcome." *Sixteen Short Stories by Outstanding Writers for Young Adults*, ed. Donald R. Gallo. New York: Dell, 1984.
"Words by Heart." *Ingenue*, December 1968, 54–55, 68–72.

Play

"Holding Out." *Center Stage: One-Act Plays for Teenage Readers and Actors*, ed. Donald R. Gallo. New York: Harper and Row, 1990.

Secondary Sources

Article

Sebestyen, Ouida. "Family Matters," *The Alan Review*, Spring 1984, 1–3.

Interview

Cline, Ruth. "A Visit with Ouida Sebestyen," *English Journal*, October, 1980, 52–53.

Speeches

Sebestyen, Ouida. "Balancing the Books," Speech given at the International Conference of the Children's Literature Association, San Diego, California, June 1990. Printed in conference proceedings, *Work and Play in Children's Literature*, eds. Susan R. Gannon and Ruth Anne Thompson, 39–44.
———. Speech given at the International Reading Association National Convention, New Orleans, Louisiana, 27 April 1981.

Film

Words by Heart, produced by Martin Tahse and adapted from the novel by Frank Dandridge; television broadcast on 11 February 1985 as part of the PBS "Wonderworks" series.

Book Reviews (Selected)

Far from Home
Booklist 15, September 1980, 111.
Bulletin of the Center for Children's Books 34, September 1980, 21.
Gauch, Patricia Lee. *New York Times Book Review* 18 January 1981, 31.
Holmstrand, James. "Novels of the Heart." *The Bloomsburg Review*, 18 January 1981, 7, 20.
Horn Book 57.1, February 1981, 60–61.

The Girl in the Box
Belden, Elizabeth A. and Judith M. Beckman. "Heroes and Victims Meet Adventure," *English Journal* 78, October 1989, 81–82.
Bulletin of the Center for Children's Books 42, September 1988, 53.
Eaglen, Audrey B. "In the YA Corner." *School Library Journal* 35, June 1989, 58.
Gallo, Donald. *English Journal* 79, September 1990, 95–96.
Horn Book 64, November/December 1988, 791.

Kirkus Reviews 56, 1 September 1988, 1328.

Publishers Weekly 234, 9 September 1988, 135.

School Library Journal 35, October 1988, 164.

Small, Robert and Susan Murphy. "Books for Adolescents," *Journal of Reading* 33, January 1990, 312.

IOU's

Abrahamson, Dick and Betty Carter. "Positive Young Adult Novels." *English Journal* 71, December 1982, 66–68.

Horn Book Magazine August 1982, 418.

Kirkus Reviews 15 April 1982, 496–97.

North, Arielle. "Of Love and Dependence." *St. Louis Post Dispatch*, 6 June 1982, n.p.

Rodowsky, Colby. "'Tis the Season for Sand Between the Pages." *Baltimore Sun*, 25 July 1982, D4.

On Fire

Booklist, 15 May 1985, 1338.

Bulletin of the Center for Children's Books, 39–40, 1985, 17.

Horn Book 61, July/August 1985, 459.

Kirkus Reviews 53, 15 May 1985, J-44.

Lewis, Marjorie. *School Library Journal* 31, April 1985, 100.

Loer, Stephanie. *The Boston Sunday Globe* 15 September 1985, 100.

Publishers Weekly 227, June 1985, 75.

Words by Heart

Beach, Fay Wilson and Glyger G. Beach. "*Words by Heart*: An Analysis of Its Theology." *Interracial Books for Children Bulletin* 11.7, 1980, 16.

Brewbaker, James. "Are You There, Margaret? It's Me, God—Religious Contexts in Recent Adolescent Literature." *English Journal* 72, September 1983, 86.

Hunter, Kristin. "Blurred View of Black Childhood." *The Washington Post*, 10 June 1979, E3.

Mercier, Jean E. "Story Behind the Book: *Words by Heart*." *Publishers Weekly*, 28 May 1979, 40.

Sims, Rudine. "*Words by Heart*: A Black Perspective." *Interracial Books for Children Bulletin* 11.7, 1980, 15.

Index

The Author

Virginia R. Monseau is Professor of English at Youngstown State University, Youngstown, Ohio, where she teaches graduate and undergraduate courses in young adult literature, children's literature, and composition. Active in the Assembly on Literature for Adolescents of the National Council of Teachers of English, she has served on its board of directors and is a past president of the organization. She has published numerous articles and book reviews about young adult literature and has co-edited and written chapters in two volumes of essays: *Missing Chapters: Ten Pioneering Women in NCTE and English Education*, and *Reading Their World: The Young Adult Novel in the Classroom*. She currently serves as co-editor of the book review column of *The ALAN Review*.

The Editor

Patricia J. (Patty) Campbell is an author and critic specializing in books for young adults. She has taught adolescent literature at University of California–Los Angeles and is the former assistant cordinator of Young Adult Services for Los Angeles Public Library. IIer literary criticism has been published in the *New York Times Book Review* and many other journals. From 1978 to 1988 her column, "The YA Perplex," a monthly review of young adult books, appeared in the *Wilson Library Bulletin*. She now writes a review column on the independent press for that magazine. Campbell is the author of five books, among them *Presenting Robert Cormier*, the first volume in the Twayne Young Adult Author Series. In 1989 she was the recipient of the American Library Association Grolier Award for distinguished achievement with young people and books. A native of Los Angeles, Campbell presently lives on an avocado ranch near San Diego, where she and her husband David Shore write and publish books on overseas camper van travel.